Just The facts101

Textbook Key Facts

Pac-Go Chemistry For General Chemistry

Table of Contents

Just The Facts101

Exam Prep for

Pac-Go Chemistry For General
Chemistry

Just The Facts101 Exam Prep is your link from
the textbook and lecture to your exams.

**Just The Facts101 Exam Preps are unauthorized and comprehensive reviews
of your textbooks.**

All material provided by CTI Publications (c) 2019

Textbook publishers and textbook authors do not participate in or contribute to these reviews.

Just The Facts101 Exam Prep

eAIN 459155

Fundamentals of Chemistry

Chemistry addresses topics such as how atoms and molecules interact via chemical bonds to form new chemical compounds. There are four types of chemical bonds: covalent bonds, in which compounds share one or more electron(s); ionic bonds, in which a compound donates one or more electrons to another compound to produce ions (cations and anions); hydrogen bonds; and Van der Waals force bonds.

:: Chemical elements ::

_____ is a chemical element with symbol Ni and atomic number 28. It is a silvery-white lustrous metal with a slight golden tinge. _____ belongs to the transition metals and is hard and ductile. Pure _____ , powdered to maximize the reactive surface area, shows a significant chemical activity, but larger pieces are slow to react with air under standard conditions because an oxide layer forms on the surface and prevents further corrosion . Even so, pure native _____ is found in Earth`s crust only in tiny amounts, usually in ultramafic rocks, and in the interiors of larger _____ —iron meteorites that were not exposed to oxygen when outside Earth`s atmosphere.

1. *Answer choices:*

(see index for correct answer)

- a. Flerovium
- b. Dubnium
- c. Neptunium
- d. Niobium

Guidance: level 1

:: Coordination chemistry ::

The _____ , sometimes referred to as oxidation number, describes the degree of oxidation of an atom in a chemical compound. Conceptually, the _____ , which may be positive, negative or zero, is the hypothetical charge that an atom would have if all bonds to atoms of different elements were 100% ionic, with no covalent component. This is never exactly true for real bonds.

Exam Probability: **Medium**

2. *Answer choices:*

(see index for correct answer)

- a. Coordination isomerism
- b. Ate complex

- c. Oxidation state
- d. Octahedral molecular geometry

Guidance: level 1

:: Concepts in physics ::

Whether electric or magnetic, _____ s can be characterized by their _____ moment, a vector quantity. For the simple electric _____ , the electric _____ moment points from the negative charge towards the positive charge, and has a magnitude equal to the strength of each charge times the separation between the charges.

Exam Probability: **Low**

3. *Answer choices:*

(see index for correct answer)

- a. Dipole
- b. wavefunction
- c. kinetic theory of gases
- d. particle

Guidance: level 1

:: Neurotoxins ::

_____ is an aromatic organic compound with the molecular formula C_6H_5OH. It is a white crystalline solid that is volatile. The molecule consists of a phenyl group bonded to a hydroxy group. It is mildly acidic and requires careful handling due to its propensity for causing chemical burns.

Exam Probability: **Medium**

4. *Answer choices:*

(see index for correct answer)

- a. Agitoxin
- b. Tertiapin
- c. Aconitum
- d. Phenol

Guidance: level 1

:: Chemical reactions ::

_____ , also known as reaction kinetics, is the study of rates of chemical processes. _____ includes investigations of how different experimental conditions can influence the speed of a chemical reaction and yield information about the reaction's mechanism and transition states, as well as the construction of mathematical models that can describe the characteristics of a chemical reaction.

Exam Probability: **High**

5. *Answer choices:*

(see index for correct answer)

- a. oxidation
- b. Chemical kinetics
- c. first-order reaction
- d. Reducing agent

Guidance: level 1

:: Chemical elements ::

_____ is a chemical element with symbol Pb and atomic number 82. It is a heavy metal that is denser than most common materials. _____ is soft and malleable, and also has a relatively low melting point. When freshly cut, _____ is silvery with a hint of blue; it tarnishes to a dull gray color when exposed to air. _____ has the highest atomic number of any stable element and three of its isotopes are endpoints of major nuclear decay chains of heavier elements.

Exam Probability: **High**

6. *Answer choices:*

(see index for correct answer)

- a. Gadolinium
- b. Fluorine
- c. Element collecting

- d. Hassium

:: Periodic table ::

A _____ is a type of chemical element which has properties in between, or that are a mixture of, those of metals and nonmetals. There is neither a standard definition of a _____ nor complete agreement on the elements appropriately classified as such. Despite the lack of specificity, the term remains in use in the literature of chemistry.

Exam Probability: **Low**

7. *Answer choices:*

(see index for correct answer)

- a. Metalloid
- b. Period 7 element
- c. Period 9 element
- d. Alkaline earth metal

:: Chemical elements ::

_____ is a chemical element with symbol I and atomic number 53. The heaviest of the stable halogens, it exists as a lustrous, purple-black non-metallic solid at standard conditions that melts to form a deep violet liquid at 114 degrees Celsius, and boils to a violet gas at 184 degrees Celsius. The element was discovered by the French chemist Bernard Courtois in 1811. It was named two years later by Joseph Louis Gay-Lussac from this property, after the Greek d "violet-coloured".

Exam Probability: **Low**

8. *Answer choices:*

(see index for correct answer)

- a. Radium
- b. Scandium
- c. Cerium
- d. Polonium

Guidance: level 1

:: Acid-base chemistry ::

An _____ is a molecule or ion capable of donating a hydron , or, alternatively, capable of forming a covalent bond with an electron pair .

Exam Probability: **Low**

9. *Answer choices:*

(see index for correct answer)

- a. Ole Siggaard-Andersen
- b. Amphichromatic
- c. Acid
- d. Pitzer ion interaction

Guidance: level 1

:: Mineral acids ::

_____ is a mineral acid with the formula $HClO_4$. Usually found as an aqueous solution, this colorless compound is a stronger acid than sulphuric acid and nitric acid. It is a powerful oxidizer when hot, but aqueous solutions up to approximately 70% by weight at room temperature are generally safe, only showing strong acid features and no oxidizing properties. _____ is useful for preparing perchlorate salts, especially ammonium perchlorate, an important rocket fuel component. _____ is dangerously corrosive and readily forms potentially explosive mixtures.

Exam Probability: **Low**

10. *Answer choices:*

(see index for correct answer)

- a. Perchloric acid
- b. Hypochlorous acid

- c. Fluorosulfuric acid
- d. Phosphoric acid

Guidance: level 1

:: Chelating agents ::

_____ is a weak organic acid that has the chemical formula $C_6H_8O_7$. It occurs naturally in citrus fruits. In biochemistry, it is an intermediate in the _____ cycle, which occurs in the metabolism of all aerobic organisms.

Exam Probability: **Medium**

11. *Answer choices:*

(see index for correct answer)

- a. Pendetide
- b. Citric acid
- c. Phytochelatin
- d. Porphin

Guidance: level 1

:: Solids ::

_____ is one of the four fundamental states of matter . In _____ s particles are closely packed. It is characterized by structural rigidity and resistance to changes of shape or volume. Unlike liquid, a _____ object does not flow to take on the shape of its container, nor does it expand to fill the entire volume available to it like a gas does. The atoms in a _____ are tightly bound to each other, either in a regular geometric lattice or irregularly . _____ s cannot be compressed with little pressure whereas gases can be compressed with little pressure because in gases molecules are loosely packed.

Exam Probability: **Low**

12. *Answer choices:*

(see index for correct answer)

- a. Triphosphorus pentanitride
- b. Solid

Guidance: level 1

:: Starch ::

_____ is a simple sugar with the molecular formula C6H12O6. _____ is the most abundant monosaccharide, a subcategory of carbohydrates. _____ is mainly made by plants and most algae during photosynthesis from water and carbon dioxide, using energy from sunlight. There it is used to make cellulose in cell walls, which is the most abundant carbohydrate. In energy metabolism, _____ is the most important source of energy in all organisms. _____ for metabolism is partially stored as a polymer, in plants mainly as starch and amylopectin and in animals as glycogen. _____ circulates in the blood of animals as blood sugar. The naturally occurring form of _____ is - _____ , while - _____ is produced synthetically in comparatively small amounts and is of lesser importance.

Exam Probability: **High**

13. *Answer choices:*

(see index for correct answer)

- a. Konnyaku
- b. Hydroxypropyl distarch phosphate
- c. Glucose
- d. Kudzu

Guidance: level 1

:: Radioactivity ::

_____ is the time required for a quantity to reduce to half its initial value. The term is commonly used in nuclear physics to describe how quickly unstable atoms undergo, or how long stable atoms survive, radioactive decay. The term is also used more generally to characterize any type of exponential or non-exponential decay. For example, the medical sciences refer to the biological _____ of drugs and other chemicals in the human body. The converse of _____ is doubling time.

Exam Probability: **Medium**

14. *Answer choices:*

(see index for correct answer)

- a. Background radiation
- b. Collective dose
- c. Cumulative dose
- d. Half-life

Guidance: level 1

:: Atmosphere of Earth ::

The _____ or ozone shield is a region of Earth's stratosphere that absorbs most of the Sun's ultraviolet radiation. It contains high concentration of ozone in relation to other parts of the atmosphere, although still small in relation to other gases in the stratosphere. The _____ contains less than 10 parts per million of ozone, while the average ozone concentration in Earth's atmosphere as a whole is about 0.3 parts per million. The _____ is mainly found in the lower portion of the stratosphere, from approximately 15 to 35 kilometers above Earth, although its thickness varies seasonally and geographically.

Exam Probability: **Low**

15. *Answer choices:*

(see index for correct answer)

- a. Thermosphere
- b. U.S. Standard Atmosphere
- c. Ozone layer
- d. Mesopause

Guidance: level 1

:: Cations ::

A _____ is a subatomic particle, symbol p or p+, with a positive electric charge of +1e elementary charge and a mass slightly less than that of a neutron. _____ s and neutrons, each with masses of approximately one atomic mass unit, are collectively referred to as "nucleons".

16. *Answer choices:*

(see index for correct answer)

- a. Trihydrogen cation
- b. Oxalyl
- c. Proton
- d. Fluoronium

Guidance: level 1

:: Polymers ::

A _____ is a large molecule, or macromolecule, composed of many repeated subunits. Due to their broad range of properties, both synthetic and natural _____ s play essential and ubiquitous roles in everyday life. _____ s range from familiar synthetic plastics such as polystyrene to natural bio _____ s such as DNA and proteins that are fundamental to biological structure and function. _____ s, both natural and synthetic, are created via _____ ization of many small molecules, known as monomers. Their consequently large molecular mass relative to small molecule compounds produces unique physical properties, including toughness, viscoelasticity, and a tendency to form glasses and semicrystalline structures rather than crystals. The terms _____ and resin are often synonymous with plastic.

Exam Probability: **High**

17. *Answer choices:*

(see index for correct answer)

- a. Polymer
- b. Silicone quaternary amine
- c. Noryl
- d. Kraton

Guidance: level 1

:: Subatomic particles ::

In the physical sciences, _____ s are particles much smaller than atoms. The two types of _____ s are: elementary particles, which according to current theories are not made of other particles; and composite particles. Particle physics and nuclear physics study these particles and how they interact. The idea of a particle underwent serious rethinking when experiments showed that light could behave like a stream of particles as well as exhibiting wave-like properties. This led to the new concept of wave–particle duality to reflect that quantum-scale "particles" behave like both particles and waves . Another new concept, the uncertainty principle, states that some of their properties taken together, such as their simultaneous position and momentum, cannot be measured exactly. In more recent times, wave–particle duality has been shown to apply not only to photons but to increasingly massive particles as well.

Exam Probability: **Medium**

18. *Answer choices:*

(see index for correct answer)

- a. Exotic hadron
- b. Subatomic particle
- c. Fermion
- d. Proton spin crisis

Guidance: level 1

:: Chemical elements ::

_____ is a chemical element with symbol Ra and atomic number 88. It is the sixth element in group 2 of the periodic table, also known as the alkaline earth metals. Pure _____ is silvery-white, but it readily reacts with nitrogen on exposure to air, forming a black surface layer of _____ nitride . All isotopes of _____ are highly radioactive, with the most stable isotope being _____ -226, which has a half-life of 1600 years and decays into radon gas . When _____ decays, ionizing radiation is a product, which can excite fluorescent chemicals and cause radioluminescence.

Exam Probability: **High**

19. *Answer choices:*

(see index for correct answer)

- a. Ununseptium
- b. Dubnium
- c. Radium
- d. Rubidium

:: Mass spectrometry ::

In physics, _____ is the minimum energy required to disassemble a system of particles into separate parts. This energy is equal to the mass defect minus the amount of energy, or mass, that is released when a bound system is created, and is what keeps the system together.

Exam Probability: **High**

20. *Answer choices:*

(see index for correct answer)

- a. Electron multiplier
- b. Kendrick mass
- c. Binding energy
- d. ISOLTRAP

:: bad_topic ::

Aluminium is a chemical element with symbol Al and atomic number 13. It is a silvery-white, soft, nonmagnetic and ductile metal in the boron group. By mass, aluminium makes up about 8% of the Earth's crust; it is the third most abundant element after oxygen and silicon and the most abundant metal in the crust, though it is less common in the mantle below. The chief ore of aluminium is bauxite. Aluminium metal is so chemically reactive that native specimens are rare and limited to extreme reducing environments. Instead, it is found combined in over 270 different minerals.

Exam Probability: **High**

21. *Answer choices:*

(see index for correct answer)

- a. Scoopula
- b. Aluminum
- c. broadband
- d. phase inversion

Guidance: level 1

:: Crystallography ::

In crystallography, _____ is a description of the ordered arrangement of atoms, ions or molecules in a crystalline material. Ordered structures occur from the intrinsic nature of the constituent particles to form symmetric patterns that repeat along the principal directions of three-dimensional space in matter.

22. *Answer choices:*

(see index for correct answer)

- a. Homeotropic alignment
- b. Reflection high-energy electron diffraction
- c. Avrami equation
- d. Crystal structure

Guidance: level 1

:: Bases ::

A _____ is a chemical species that contains an empty orbital which is capable of accepting an electron pair from a Lewis base to form a Lewis adduct. A Lewis base, then, is any species that has a filled orbital containing an electron pair which is not involved in bonding but may form a dative bond with a _____ to form a Lewis adduct. For example, NH_3 is a Lewis base, because it can donate its lone pair of electrons. Trimethylborane is a _____ as it is capable of accepting a lone pair. In a Lewis adduct, the _____ and base share an electron pair furnished by the Lewis base, forming a dative bond. In the context of a specific chemical reaction between NH_3 and Me_3B, the lone pair from NH_3 will form a dative bond with the empty orbital of Me_3B to form an adduct $NH_3 \cdot BMe_3$. The terminology refers to the contributions of Gilbert N. Lewis.

23. *Answer choices:*

(see index for correct answer)

- a. Lithium tetramethylpiperidide
- b. Base
- c. Potassium tert-butoxide
- d. Lewis acid

Guidance: level 1

:: Optics ::

The _____ is a type of elementary particle, the quantum of the electromagnetic field including electromagnetic radiation such as light, and the force carrier for the electromagnetic force . Invariant mass of the _____ is zero; it always moves at the speed of light within a vacuum.

Exam Probability: **Low**

24. *Answer choices:*

(see index for correct answer)

- a. Index-matching material
- b. Photon
- c. Polarization rotator
- d. Angle-resolved low-coherence interferometry

:: Noble gases ::

The _____ es make up a group of chemical elements with similar properties; under standard conditions, they are all odorless, colorless, monatomic gases with very low chemical reactivity. The six _____ es that occur naturally are helium , neon , argon , krypton , xenon , and the radioactive radon . Oganesson is variously predicted to be a _____ as well or to break the trend due to relativistic effects; its chemistry has not yet been investigated.

Exam Probability: **Medium**

25. *Answer choices:*
(see index for correct answer)

- a. William Ramsay
- b. Noble gas

Guidance: level 1

:: Mineral acids ::

_____ or muriatic acid is a colorless inorganic chemical system with the formula H2O:HCl. _____ has a distinctive pungent smell. It is classified as strongly acidic and can attack the skin over a wide composition range, since the hydrogen chloride completely dissociates in aqueous solution.

Exam Probability: **Medium**

26. *Answer choices:*

(see index for correct answer)

- a. Hydrochloric acid
- b. Aqua regia
- c. Mineral acid
- d. Chloric acid

Guidance: level 1

:: Atomic physics ::

In quantum mechanics, the _____ is one of four quantum numbers which are assigned to all electrons in an atom to describe that electron's state. As a discrete variable, the _____ is always an integer. As n increases, the number of electronic shells increases and the electron spends more time farther from the nucleus. As n increases, the electron is also at a higher energy and is, therefore, less tightly bound to the nucleus. The total energy of an electron, as described below, is a negative inverse quadratic function of the _____ n.

27. *Answer choices:*

(see index for correct answer)

- a. Uncleftish Beholding
- b. Principal quantum number
- c. Electron configuration
- d. Radiative Auger effect

Guidance: level 1

:: Spectroscopy ::

_____ is the study of the interaction between matter and electromagnetic radiation. Historically, _____ originated through the study of visible light dispersed according to its wavelength, by a prism. Later the concept was expanded greatly to include any interaction with radiative energy as a function of its wavelength or frequency, predominantly in the electromagnetic spectrum, though matter waves and acoustic waves can also be considered forms of radiative energy; recently, with tremendous difficulty, even gravitational waves have been associated with a spectral signature in the context of LIGO and laser interferometry. Spectroscopic data are often represented by an emission spectrum, a plot of the response of interest as a function of wavelength or frequency.

Exam Probability: **Low**

28. *Answer choices:*

(see index for correct answer)

- a. History of spectroscopy
- b. Spectroscopy
- c. Chemiluminescence
- d. Acoustic paramagnetic resonance

Guidance: level 1

:: Ethers ::

_____ , or simply ether, is an organic compound in the ether class with the formula 2O, sometimes abbreviated as Et2O . It is a colorless, highly volatile flammable liquid. It is commonly used as a solvent in laboratories and as a starting fluid for some engines. It was formerly used as a general anesthetic, until non-flammable drugs were developed, such as halothane. It has been used as a recreational drug to cause intoxication.

Exam Probability: **Medium**

29. *Answer choices:*
(see index for correct answer)

- a. Fenticonazole
- b. DBL-583
- c. Diethyl ether
- d. Setastine

Guidance: level 1

:: Quantum mechanics ::

The _________ of a quantum-mechanical system is its lowest-energy state; the energy of the _________ is known as the zero-point energy of the system. An is any state with energy greater than the _________ . In the quantum field theory, the _________ is usually called the vacuum state or the vacuum.

Exam Probability: **Medium**

30. *Answer choices:*

(see index for correct answer)

- a. Coherent states
- b. Quantum gyroscope
- c. Ground state
- d. Gyrovector space

Guidance: level 1

:: Radioactivity ::

_____ is the process by which an unstable atomic nucleus loses energy by emitting radiation, such as an alpha particle, beta particle with neutrino or only a neutrino in the case of electron capture, or a gamma ray or electron in the case of internal conversion. A material containing such unstable nuclei is considered radioactive. Certain highly excited short-lived nuclear states can decay through neutron emission, or more rarely, proton emission.

Exam Probability: **High**

31. *Answer choices:*

(see index for correct answer)

- a. CD V-700
- b. Decay chain
- c. Critical mass
- d. Radioactive decay

Guidance: level 1

:: Physical chemistry ::

An _____ is a substance that produces an electrically conducting solution when dissolved in a polar solvent, such as water. The dissolved _____ separates into cations and anions, which disperse uniformly through the solvent. Electrically, such a solution is neutral. If an electric potential is applied to such a solution, the cations of the solution are drawn to the electrode that has an abundance of electrons, while the anions are drawn to the electrode that has a deficit of electrons. The movement of anions and cations in opposite directions within the solution amounts to a current. This includes most soluble salts, acids, and bases. Some gases, such as hydrogen chloride, under conditions of high temperature or low pressure can also function as _____ s. _____ solutions can also result from the dissolution of some biological and synthetic polymers , termed "poly _____ s", which contain charged functional groups. A substance that dissociates into ions in solution acquires the capacity to conduct electricity. Sodium, potassium, chloride, calcium, magnesium, and phosphate are examples of _____ s.

Exam Probability: **Medium**

32. *Answer choices:*

(see index for correct answer)

- a. Eyring equation
- b. E. Bright Wilson Award in Spectroscopy
- c. Electron transfer
- d. Solidus

Guidance: level 1

:: Organic chemistry ::

_____ s , also called simple sugar, are the simplest form of sugar and the most basic units of carbohydrates. They cannot be further hydrolyzed to simpler chemical compounds. The general formula is $C_nH_{2n}O_n$. They are usually colorless, water-soluble, and crystalline solids. Some _____ s have a sweet taste.

Exam Probability: **High**

33. *Answer choices:*

(see index for correct answer)

- a. Extract
- b. N-linked glycosylation
- c. FAD dependent oxidoreductase family
- d. Monosaccharide

Guidance: level 1

:: Animal products ::

_____ is a peptide hormone produced by beta cells of the pancreatic islets; it is considered to be the main anabolic hormone of the body. It regulates the metabolism of carbohydrates, fats and protein by promoting the absorption of carbohydrates, especially glucose from the blood into liver, fat and skeletal muscle cells. In these tissues the absorbed glucose is converted into either glycogen via glycogenesis or fats via lipogenesis, or, in the case of the liver, into both. Glucose production and secretion by the liver is strongly inhibited by high concentrations of _____ in the blood. Circulating _____ also affects the synthesis of proteins in a wide variety of tissues. It is therefore an anabolic hormone, promoting the conversion of small molecules in the blood into large molecules inside the cells. Low _____ levels in the blood have the opposite effect by promoting widespread catabolism, especially of reserve body fat.

Exam Probability: **High**

34. *Answer choices:*

(see index for correct answer)

- a. Colostrum
- b. Bile bear
- c. Insulin
- d. Animal source foods

Guidance: level 1

:: Separation processes ::

_____ is the process of separating the components or substances from a liquid mixture by using selective boiling and condensation. _____ may result in essentially complete separation , or it may be a partial separation that increases the concentration of selected components in the mixture. In either case, the process exploits differences in the volatility of the mixture's components. In industrial chemistry, _____ is a unit operation of practically universal importance, but it is a physical separation process, not a chemical reaction.

Exam Probability: **Low**

35. *Answer choices:*

(see index for correct answer)

- a. Crystallization of polymers
- b. Distillation
- c. Flotation process
- d. Expeller pressing

Guidance: level 1

:: Alkylbenzenes ::

_____ , also known as toluol , is an aromatic hydrocarbon. It is a colorless, water-insoluble liquid with the smell associated with paint thinners. It is a mono-substituted benzene derivative, consisting of a CH3 group attached to a phenyl group. As such, its IUPAC systematic name is methylbenzene. _____ is predominantly used as an industrial feedstock and a solvent.

36. *Answer choices:*

(see index for correct answer)

- a. Dodecylbenzene
- b. Toluene
- c. Alkylbenzenes
- d. Linear alkylbenzene

Guidance: level 1

:: Inorganic compounds ::

_____ , also known as lye and caustic soda, is an inorganic compound with the formula NaOH. It is a white solid ionic compound consisting of sodium cations Na+ and hydroxide anions OH-.

Exam Probability: **High**

37. *Answer choices:*

(see index for correct answer)

- a. Potassium sulfide
- b. Acidifier
- c. Sodium hydroxide
- d. Hydrogen cyanide

- a. Fanjul brothers
- b. Simple Sugars
- c. Nib sugar
- d. Sucrose

Guidance: level 1

:: Chemical elements ::

_____ is a chemical element with symbol P and atomic number 15. Elemental _____ exists in two major forms, white _____ and red _____ , but because it is highly reactive, _____ is never found as a free element on Earth. It has a concentration in the Earth's crust of about one gram per kilogram . With few exceptions, minerals containing _____ are in the maximally oxidized state as inorganic phosphate rocks.

Exam Probability: **High**

43. *Answer choices:*

- a. Zinc
- b. Nobelium
- c. Roentgenium
- d. Phosphorus

:: Oxidizing agents ::

In chemistry, an _____ is a substance that has the ability to oxidize other substances—in other words to cause them to lose electrons. Common _____ s are oxygen, hydrogen peroxide and the halogens.

Exam Probability: **Low**

44. *Answer choices:*

(see index for correct answer)

- a. Tetrapropylammonium perruthenate
- b. Potassium trioxochlorochromate
- c. Oxidizing agent
- d. Silver bromate

:: Functional groups ::

In organic chemistry, an _____ is an unsaturated hydrocarbon that contains at least one carbon–carbon double bond. The words _____ and olefin are often used interchangeably . Acyclic _____ s, with only one double bond and no other functional groups, known as mono-enes, form a homologous series of hydrocarbons with the general formula $CnH2n$. _____ s have two hydrogen atoms fewer than the corresponding alkane . The simplest _____ , ethylene , with the International Union of Pure and Applied Chemistry name ethene, is the organic compound produced on the largest scale industrially. Aromatic compounds are often drawn as cyclic _____ s, but their structure and properties are different and they are not considered to be _____ s.

Exam Probability: **Medium**

45. *Answer choices:*

(see index for correct answer)

- a. Nitrile ylide
- b. Carboximidate
- c. Enyne
- d. Alkene

Guidance: level 1

:: Catalysis ::

_____ s are macromolecular biological catalysts. _____ s accelerate chemical reactions. The molecules upon which _____ s may act are called substrates and the _____ converts the substrates into different molecules known as products. Almost all metabolic processes in the cell need _____ catalysis in order to occur at rates fast enough to sustain life. Metabolic pathways depend upon _____ s to catalyze individual steps. The study of _____ s is called enzymology and a new field of pseudo _____ analysis has recently grown up, recognising that during evolution, some _____ s have lost the ability to carry out biological catalysis, which is often reflected in their amino acid sequences and unusual `pseudocatalytic` properties.

Exam Probability: **Medium**

46. *Answer choices:*

(see index for correct answer)

- a. Thiele modulus
- b. Cuprospinel
- c. Enzyme
- d. Andrussow process

Guidance: level 1

:: Limestone ::

_____ is a chemical compound with the formula CaCO3. It is a common substance found in rocks as the minerals and aragonite and is the main component of pearls and the shells of marine organisms, snails, and eggs.

_____ is the active ingredient in agricultural lime and is created when calcium ions in hard water react with carbonate ions to create limescale. It is medicinally used as a calcium supplement or as an antacid, but excessive consumption can be hazardous.

Exam Probability: **Medium**

47. *Answer choices:*

(see index for correct answer)

- a. Ashford Black Marble
- b. Charlestown limestone
- c. Istrian stone
- d. Calcium carbonate

Guidance: level 1

:: Sterols ::

_____ is an organic molecule. It is a sterol , a type of lipid.
_____ is biosynthesized by all animal cells and is an essential structural component of animal cell membranes.

Exam Probability: **Medium**

48. *Answer choices:*

(see index for correct answer)

- a. Spinasterol
- b. Ergosterol
- c. 5-Dehydroepisterol
- d. Cholesterol

Guidance: level 1

:: Atomic physics ::

In physics and chemistry, _____ or ionisation energy , denoted Ei, is the minimum amount of energy required to remove the most loosely bound electron, the valence electron, of an isolated neutral gaseous atom or molecule. It is quantitatively expressed as

Exam Probability: **High**

49. *Answer choices:*

(see index for correct answer)

- a. Atomic theory
- b. Mirror nuclei
- c. X-ray notation
- d. Transition dipole moment

:: Inorganic chemistry ::

In chemistry, an _____ is a basic, ionic salt of an _____ metal or _____ ne earth metal chemical element. An _____ also can be defined as a base that dissolves in water. A solution of a soluble base has a pH greater than 7.0. The adjective _____ ne is commonly, and alkalescent less often, used in English as a synonym for basic, especially for bases soluble in water. This broad use of the term is likely to have come about because _____ s were the first bases known to obey the Arrhenius definition of a base, and they are still among the most common bases.

Exam Probability: **High**

50. *Answer choices:*

(see index for correct answer)

- a. Nucleophilic abstraction
- b. Alkali
- c. Homoleptic
- d. Bioinorganic chemistry

Guidance: level 1

:: Optical materials ::

_____ is a chemical element with symbol Ge and atomic number 32. It is a lustrous, hard-brittle, grayish-white metalloid in the carbon group, chemically similar to its group neighbours silicon and tin. Pure _____ is a semiconductor with an appearance similar to elemental silicon. Like silicon, _____ naturally reacts and forms complexes with oxygen in nature.

Exam Probability: **Medium**

51. *Answer choices:*

(see index for correct answer)

- a. Zinc selenide
- b. Germanium
- c. Uniformity tape
- d. Polycarbonate

Guidance: level 1

:: Nuclear physics ::

_____ or beta plus decay is a subtype of radioactive decay called beta decay, in which a proton inside a radionuclide nucleus is converted into a neutron while releasing a positron and an electron neutrino . _____ is mediated by the weak force. The positron is a type of beta particle , the other beta particle being the electron emitted from the ß- decay of a nucleus.

Exam Probability: **Low**

Answer choices:

(see index for correct answer)

- a. Spontaneous fission
- b. Binary collision approximation
- c. P-nuclei
- d. S-process

Guidance: level 1

:: Solutions ::

_____ is the minimum pressure which needs to be applied to a solution to prevent the inward flow of its pure solvent across a semipermeable membrane. It is also defined as the measure of the tendency of a solution to take in pure solvent by osmosis. Potential _____ is the maximum _____ that could develop in a solution if it were separated from its pure solvent by a semipermeable membrane.

Exam Probability: **Medium**

53. *Answer choices:*

(see index for correct answer)

- a. Osmolyte
- b. Solvation shell
- c. Osmotic pressure
- d. Aqueous solution

:: Chemical reactions ::

A _____ is an element or compound that loses an electron to another chemical species in a redox chemical reaction. Since the _____ is losing electrons, it is said to have been oxidized.

Exam Probability: **Medium**

54. *Answer choices:*

(see index for correct answer)

- a. Chloro-5-substituted adamantyl-1,2-dioxetane phosphate
- b. Potentiator
- c. Chemoselectivity
- d. Auxochrome

:: Chemical elements ::

_____ is the chemical element with the symbol O and atomic number 8. It is a member of the chalcogen group on the periodic table, a highly reactive nonmetal, and an oxidizing agent that readily forms oxides with most elements as well as with other compounds. By mass, _____ is the third-most abundant element in the universe, after hydrogen and helium. At standard temperature and pressure, two atoms of the element bind to form di _____ , a colorless and odorless diatomic gas with the formula O2. Diatomic _____ gas constitutes 20.8% of the Earth`s atmosphere. As compounds including oxides, the element makes up almost half of the Earth`s crust.

Exam Probability: **High**

55. *Answer choices:*

(see index for correct answer)

- a. Actinium
- b. Oxygen
- c. Hydrogen
- d. Lanthanum

Guidance: level 1

:: Materials science ::

_____ is a type of vaporization that occurs on the surface of a liquid as it changes into the gas phase. The surrounding gas must not be saturated with the evaporating substance. When the molecules of the liquid collide, they transfer energy to each other based on how they collide with each other. When a molecule near the surface absorbs enough energy to overcome the vapor pressure, it will escape and enter the surrounding air as a gas. When _____ occurs, the energy removed from the vaporized liquid will reduce the temperature of the liquid, resulting in evaporative cooling.

Exam Probability: **High**

56. *Answer choices:*

(see index for correct answer)

- a. Frank-Read Source
- b. Archard equation
- c. Friability
- d. Evaporation

Guidance: level 1

:: Mineral acids ::

_____ , also known as vitriol, is a mineral acid composed of the elements sulfur, oxygen and hydrogen, with molecular formula H_2SO_4. It is a colorless, odorless, and syrupy liquid that is soluble in water and is synthesized in reactions that are highly exothermic.

57. *Answer choices:*

(see index for correct answer)

- a. Nitric acid
- b. Hydrobromic acid
- c. Silicic acid
- d. Sulfuric acid

Guidance: level 1

:: Functional groups ::

_____ s are a class of organic compounds that contain an _____ group—an oxygen atom connected to two alkyl or aryl groups. They have the general formula R–O–R', where R and R' represent the alkyl or aryl groups. _____ s can again be classified into two varieties: if the alkyl groups are the same on both sides of the oxygen atom, then it is a simple or symmetrical _____ , whereas if they are different, the _____ s are called mixed or unsymmetrical _____ s. A typical example of the first group is the solvent and anesthetic diethyl _____ , commonly referred to simply as " _____ ". _____ s are common in organic chemistry and even more prevalent in biochemistry, as they are common linkages in carbohydrates and lignin.

Exam Probability: **Low**

58. *Answer choices:*

(see index for correct answer)

- a. Aziridine
- b. Ether
- c. Sulfilimine
- d. Alkene

Guidance: level 1

:: Household chemicals ::

_____ is an organic compound with the formula 2. It is mainly used for two purposes, as a raw material in the manufacture of polyester fibers and for antifreeze formulations. It is an odorless, colorless, sweet-tasting, viscous liquid. _____ is toxic. Household pets are especially susceptible to _____ poisoning from vehicle antifreeze leaks.

Exam Probability: **High**

59. *Answer choices:*
(see index for correct answer)

- a. Insect repellent
- b. Camphine
- c. DEET
- d. Sodium lauroyl sarcosinate

Guidance: level 1

Materials science

The interdisciplinary field of materials science, also commonly termed
materials science and engineering is the design and discovery of new materials,
particularly solids. The intellectual origins of materials science stem from
the Enlightenment, when researchers began to use analytical thinking from
chemistry, physics, and engineering to understand ancient, phenomenological
observations in metallurgy and mineralogy.[1][2] Materials science still
incorporates elements of physics, chemistry, and engineering.

:: Atomic physics ::

_____ is the ability to form instantaneous dipoles. It is a property of
matter. Polarizabilities determine the dynamical response of a bound system to
external fields, and provide insight into a molecule's internal structure. In a
solid, _____ is defined as dipole moment per unit volume of the crystal
cell.

Exam Probability: **High**

1. *Answer choices:*

(see index for correct answer)

- a. Electron beam ion trap
- b. Resolved sideband cooling
- c. Electronic density
- d. Polarizability

Guidance: level 1

:: Electric and magnetic fields in matter ::

A _____ is an electrical insulator that can be polarized by an applied electric field. When a _____ is placed in an electric field, electric charges do not flow through the material as they do in an electrical conductor but only slightly shift from their average equilibrium positions causing _____ polarization. Because of _____ polarization, positive charges are displaced in the direction of the field and negative charges shift in the opposite direction. This creates an internal electric field that reduces the overall field within the _____ itself. If a _____ is composed of weakly bonded molecules, those molecules not only become polarized, but also reorient so that their symmetry axes align to the field.

Exam Probability: **Low**

2. *Answer choices:*

(see index for correct answer)

- a. Magnetization

- b. Dielectric
- c. Magneto-optic effect
- d. Polarization density

Guidance: level 1

:: Equilibrium chemistry ::

_____ is a term used for both an electro-chemical process and a biological one. The _____ of water is the separation of water molecules into hydrogen and oxygen atoms using electricity .

Exam Probability: **High**

3. *Answer choices:*

(see index for correct answer)

- a. Pitzer equations
- b. Hydrolysis
- c. Fugacity capacity
- d. Aminopolycarboxylic acid

Guidance: level 1

:: Materials science ::

A _____ is a light-sensitive material used in several processes, such as photolithography and photoengraving, to form a patterned coating on a surface. This process is crucial in the electronic industry.

Exam Probability: **High**

4. *Answer choices:*

(see index for correct answer)

- a. Electron mobility
- b. Photoresist
- c. Goodman relation
- d. Terahertz nondestructive evaluation

Guidance: level 1

:: Composite materials ::

_____ is a composite material in which concrete's relatively low tensile strength and ductility are counteracted by the inclusion of reinforcement having higher tensile strength or ductility. The reinforcement is usually, though not necessarily, steel reinforcing bars and is usually embedded passively in the concrete before the concrete sets. Reinforcing schemes are generally designed to resist tensile stresses in particular regions of the concrete that might cause unacceptable cracking and/or structural failure. Modern _____ can contain varied reinforcing materials made of steel, polymers or alternate composite material in conjunction with rebar or not. _____ may also be permanently stressed , so as to improve the behaviour of the final structure under working loads. In the United States, the most common methods of doing this are known as pre-tensioning and post-tensioning.

Exam Probability: **Medium**

5. *Answer choices:*

(see index for correct answer)

- a. Glidcop
- b. Reinforced concrete
- c. Fiber cement siding
- d. Pykrete

Guidance: level 1

:: Statics ::

In statics, a structure is _____ when the static equilibrium equations are insufficient for determining the internal forces and reactions on that structure.

Exam Probability: **Low**

6. *Answer choices:*

(see index for correct answer)

- a. Normal force
- b. Statically indeterminate
- c. Statics
- d. Block-stacking problem

Guidance: level 1

:: Dielectrics ::

_____ or polythene is the most common plastic. As of 2017, over 100 million tonnes of _____ resins are produced annually, accounting for 34% of the total plastics market. Its primary use is in packaging . Many kinds of _____ are known, with most having the chemical formula n. PE is usually a mixture of similar polymers of ethylene with various values of n. _____ is a thermoplastic; however, it can become a thermoset plastic when modified .

Exam Probability: **Low**

7. *Answer choices:*

(see index for correct answer)

- a. Polypropylene
- b. Mica
- c. Plasma pencil
- d. Fishpaper

Guidance: level 1

:: Metallurgical processes ::

_____ process metals are plastically deformed above their recrystallization temperature. Being above the recrystallization temperature allows the material to recrystallize during deformation. This is important because recrystallization keeps the materials from strain hardening, which ultimately keeps the yield strength and hardness low and ductility high. This contrasts with cold working.

Exam Probability: **Medium**

8. *Answer choices:*

(see index for correct answer)

- a. Copper extraction techniques
- b. Hot working
- c. Carbon in pulp
- d. Electroforming

:: Polymerization reactions ::

Note:If the monomer is polycyclic, the opening of a single ring is sufficient to classify the reaction as _____ .

Exam Probability: **Low**

9. *Answer choices:*

(see index for correct answer)

- a. Step-growth polymerization
- b. Solution polymerization
- c. Ring-opening polymerization
- d. Acyclic diene metathesis

:: Chemical mixtures ::

Homogeneity and heterogeneity are concepts often used in the sciences and statistics relating to the uniformity in a substance or organism. A material or image that is _____ is uniform in composition or character ; one that is heterogeneous is distinctly nonuniform in one of these qualities.

10. *Answer choices:*

(see index for correct answer)

- a. Homogeneous
- b. Creosote
- c. Sunscreen
- d. Neutra Phos

Guidance: level 1

:: Elasticity (physics) ::

Ultimate _____ , often shortened to _____ , ultimate strength, or Ftu within equations, is the capacity of a material or structure to withstand loads tending to elongate, as opposed to compressive strength, which withstands loads tending to reduce size. In other words, _____ resists tension , whereas compressive strength resists compression . Ultimate _____ is measured by the maximum stress that a material can withstand while being stretched or pulled before breaking. In the study of strength of materials, _____ , compressive strength, and shear strength can be analyzed independently.

11. *Answer choices:*

(see index for correct answer)

- a. Seismic anisotropy
- b. Tensile strength
- c. Finite strain theory
- d. Michell solution

Guidance: level 1

:: Composite materials ::

_____ is a continuous process for manufacture of composite materials with constant cross-section. The term is a portmanteau word, combining "pull" and "extrusion". As opposed to extrusion, which pushes the material, _____ works by pulling the material.

Exam Probability: **Low**

12. *Answer choices:*

(see index for correct answer)

- a. Cadec-online.com
- b. Royalex
- c. Delamination
- d. Short fiber reinforced blends

Guidance: level 1

:: Raman spectroscopy ::

_____ ; named after Indian physicist Sir C. V. Raman) is a spectroscopic technique used to observe vibrational, rotational, and other low-frequency modes in a system. _____ is commonly used in chemistry to provide a structural fingerprint by which molecules can be identified.

Exam Probability: **High**

13. *Answer choices:*

(see index for correct answer)

- a. Surface-enhanced Raman spectroscopy
- b. Raman spectroscopy
- c. Transmission Raman spectroscopy
- d. Raman optical activity

Guidance: level 1

:: Catalysis ::

_____ s are macromolecular biological catalysts. _____ s accelerate chemical reactions. The molecules upon which _____ s may act are called substrates and the _____ converts the substrates into different molecules known as products. Almost all metabolic processes in the cell need _____ catalysis in order to occur at rates fast enough to sustain life. Metabolic pathways depend upon _____ s to catalyze individual steps. The study of _____ s is called enzymology and a new field of pseudo _____ analysis has recently grown up, recognising that during evolution, some _____ s have lost the ability to carry out biological catalysis, which is often reflected in their amino acid sequences and unusual `pseudocatalytic` properties.

Exam Probability: **High**

14. *Answer choices:*

(see index for correct answer)

- a. Catalyst support
- b. Soai reaction
- c. Active site
- d. Enzyme

Guidance: level 1

:: Crystallography ::

In physics, the _____ represents the Fourier transform of another lattice . In normal usage, this first lattice is usually a periodic spatial function in real-space and is also known as the direct lattice. While the direct lattice exists in real-space and is what one would commonly understand as a physical lattice, the _____ exists in reciprocal space The reciprocal of a _____ is the original direct lattice, since the two are Fourier transforms of each other.

Exam Probability: **High**

15. *Answer choices:*

(see index for correct answer)

- a. Sayre equation
- b. Reciprocal lattice
- c. Periodic graph
- d. Orientational glass

Guidance: level 1

:: Ceramic materials ::

_____ s have an amorphous phase and one or more crystalline phases and are produced by a so-called "controlled crystallization" in contrast to a spontaneous crystallization, which is usually not wanted in glass manufacturing. _____ s have the fabrication advantage of glass, as well as special properties of ceramics. When used for sealing, some _____ s do not require brazing but can withstand brazing temperatures up to 700 °C. _____ s usually have between 30% [m/m] and 90% [m/m] crystallinity and yield an array of materials with interesting properties like zero porosity, high strength, toughness, translucency or opacity, pigmentation, opalescence, low or even negative thermal expansion, high temperature stability, fluorescence, machinability, ferromagnetism, resorbability or high chemical durability, biocompatibility, bioactivity, ion conductivity, superconductivity, isolation capabilities, low dielectric constant and loss, high resistivity and break-down voltage. These properties can be tailored by controlling the base-glass composition and by controlled heat treatment/crystallization of base glass. In manufacturing, _____ s are valued for having the strength of ceramic but the hermetic sealing properties of glass.

Exam Probability: **High**

16. *Answer choices:*

(see index for correct answer)

- a. Silicon boride
- b. Glass-ceramic
- c. Terracotta
- d. Silicon carbide

Guidance: level 1

:: Electric and magnetic fields in matter ::

In classical electromagnetism, _____ or magnetic polarization is the vector field that expresses the density of permanent or induced magnetic dipole moments in a magnetic material. The origin of the magnetic moments responsible for _____ can be either microscopic electric currents resulting from the motion of electrons in atoms, or the spin of the electrons or the nuclei. Net _____ results from the response of a material to an external magnetic field, together with any unbalanced magnetic dipole moments that may be inherent in the material itself; for example, in ferromagnets. _____ is not always uniform within a body, but rather varies between different points. _____ also describes how a material responds to an applied magnetic field as well as the way the material changes the magnetic field, and can be used to calculate the forces that result from those interactions. It can be compared to electric polarization, which is the measure of the corresponding response of a material to an electric field in electrostatics. Physicists and engineers usually define _____ as the quantity of magnetic moment per unit volume. It is represented by a pseudovector M.

Exam Probability: **Low**

17. *Answer choices:*

(see index for correct answer)

- a. Permeance
- b. Neutron magnetic moment
- c. Magnetization
- d. Fast ion conductor

Guidance: level 1

:: Corrosion ::

_____ is a loss of ductility of a material, making it brittle. Various materials have different mechanisms of _____ .

Exam Probability: **Medium**

18. *Answer choices:*

(see index for correct answer)

- a. Internal oxidation
- b. Corrosion fatigue
- c. Polymer degradation
- d. Embrittlement

Guidance: level 1

:: Crystals ::

A _____ or _____ line solid is a solid material whose constituents are arranged in a highly ordered microscopic structure, forming a _____ lattice that extends in all directions. In addition, macroscopic single _____ s are usually identifiable by their geometrical shape, consisting of flat faces with specific, characteristic orientations. The scientific study of _____ s and _____ formation is known as _____ lography. The process of _____ formation via mechanisms of _____ growth is called _____ lization or solidification.

Exam Probability: **Low**

19. *Answer choices:*

(see index for correct answer)

- a. Debye frequency
- b. Crystal
- c. Monocrystalline silicon
- d. Anisodesmic crystal

Guidance: level 1

:: Materials science ::

_____ is a wide group of analysis techniques used in science and technology industry to evaluate the properties of a material, component or system without causing damage. The terms nondestructive examination , nondestructive inspection , and nondestructive evaluation are also commonly used to describe this technology. Because NDT does not permanently alter the article being inspected, it is a highly valuable technique that can save both money and time in product evaluation, troubleshooting, and research. The six most frequently used NDT methods are eddy-current, magnetic-particle, liquid penetrant, radiographic, ultrasonic, and visual testing. NDT is commonly used in forensic engineering, mechanical engineering, petroleum engineering, electrical engineering, civil engineering, systems engineering, aeronautical engineering, medicine, and art. Innovations in the field of _____ have had a profound impact on medical imaging, including on echocardiography, medical ultrasonography, and digital radiography.

Exam Probability: **Medium**

20. *Answer choices:*

(see index for correct answer)

- a. Nondestructive testing
- b. Digital image correlation
- c. Stress field
- d. Coulomb explosion

Guidance: level 1

:: Condensed matter physics ::

A _____ is a line graph that represents the change of phase of matter, typically from a gas to a solid or a liquid to a solid. The independent variable is time and the dependent variable is temperature. Below is an example of a _____ used in castings.

Exam Probability: **Medium**

21. *Answer choices:*
(see index for correct answer)

- a. Semimetal
- b. Ferromagnetic resonance
- c. Swift heavy ion
- d. Oliver E. Buckley Condensed Matter Prize

Guidance: level 1

:: Household chemicals ::

_____ is an organic compound with the formula 2. It is mainly used for two purposes, as a raw material in the manufacture of polyester fibers and for antifreeze formulations. It is an odorless, colorless, sweet-tasting, viscous liquid. _____ is toxic. Household pets are especially susceptible to _____ poisoning from vehicle antifreeze leaks.

Exam Probability: **Low**

22. *Answer choices:*

(see index for correct answer)

- a. Windex
- b. Glycerol
- c. Ethylene glycol
- d. Turpentine

Guidance: level 1

:: Porous media ::

_____ s are microporous, aluminosilicate minerals commonly used as commercial adsorbents and catalysts. The term _____ was originally coined in 1756 by Swedish mineralogist Axel Fredrik Cronstedt, who observed that rapidly heating the material, believed to have been stilbite, produced large amounts of steam from water that had been adsorbed by the material. Based on this, he called the material _____ , from the Greek , meaning "to boil" and , meaning "stone". The classic reference for the field has been Breck`s book _____ Molecular Sieves: Structure, Chemistry, And Use.

Exam Probability: **Medium**

23. *Answer choices:*

(see index for correct answer)

- a. Zeolite
- b. Blake number
- c. Conjugated microporous polymer
- d. Mesoporous organosilica

Guidance: level 1

:: Glass engineering and science ::

The _____ of a fluid is a measure of its resistance to deformation at a given rate. For liquids, it corresponds to the informal concept of "thickness": for example, syrup has a higher _____ than water.

Exam Probability: **Medium**

24. *Answer choices:*

(see index for correct answer)

- a. Viscosity
- b. Lehr
- c. Applied element method
- d. Heated glass

Guidance: level 1

:: Solid-state chemistry ::

_____ is a multiphase solid material where one of the phases has one, two or three dimensions of less than 100 nanometers , or structures having nano-scale repeat distances between the different phases that make up the material.

Exam Probability: **Medium**

25. *Answer choices:*

(see index for correct answer)

- a. Dangling bond
- b. Off-center ions
- c. Nanocomposite
- d. Magnetic structure

:: Anions ::

An _____ is a chemical compound that contains at least one oxygen atom and one other element in its chemical formula. " _____ " itself is the dianion of oxygen, an O2– atom. Metal _____ s thus typically contain an anion of oxygen in the oxidation state of -2. Most of the Earth`s crust consists of solid _____ s, the result of elements being oxidized by the oxygen in air or in water. Hydrocarbon combustion affords the two principal carbon _____ s: carbon mon _____ and carbon di _____ . Even materials considered pure elements often develop an _____ coating. For example, aluminium foil develops a thin skin of Al2O3 that protects the foil from further corrosion. Individual elements can often form multiple _____ s, each containing different amounts of the element and oxygen. In some cases these are distinguished by specifying the number of atoms as in carbon mon _____ and carbon di _____ , and in other cases by specifying the element`s oxidation number, as in iron _____ and iron _____ . Certain elements can form many different _____ s, such as those of nitrogen.

Exam Probability: **High**

26. *Answer choices:*

(see index for correct answer)

- a. Oxide
- b. Carbanion
- c. Metallate
- d. Borohydride

:: Steels ::

_____ refers to a variety of carbon and alloy steels that are particularly well-suited to be made into tools. Their suitability comes from their distinctive hardness, resistance to abrasion and deformation, and their ability to hold a cutting edge at elevated temperatures. As a result, _____ s are suited for use in the shaping of other materials.

Exam Probability: **High**

27. *Answer choices:*

(see index for correct answer)

- a. A36 steel
- b. Hardened steel
- c. Tool steel
- d. Dual-phase steel

:: Chemical elements ::

_____ is a chemical element with symbol Mg and atomic number 12. It is a shiny gray solid which bears a close physical resemblance to the other five elements in the second column of the periodic table: all group 2 elements have the same electron configuration in the outer electron shell and a similar crystal structure.

Exam Probability: **Medium**

28. *Answer choices:*

(see index for correct answer)

- a. Neptunium
- b. Terbium
- c. Magnesium
- d. Unbiquadium

Guidance: level 1

:: Chemical elements ::

_____ is a chemical element with symbol H and atomic number 1. With a standard atomic weight of 1.008, _____ is the lightest element in the periodic table. _____ is the most abundant chemical substance in the Universe, constituting roughly 75% of all baryonic mass. Non-remnant stars are mainly composed of _____ in the plasma state. The most common isotope of _____ , termed protium , has one proton and no neutrons.

Exam Probability: **High**

29. *Answer choices:*

(see index for correct answer)

- a. Berkelium
- b. Neon
- c. Hydrogen
- d. Lutetium

Guidance: level 1

:: Titanium alloys ::

_____ s are metals that contain a mixture of titanium and other chemical elements. Such alloys have very high tensile strength and toughness . They are light in weight, have extraordinary corrosion resistance and the ability to withstand extreme temperatures. However, the high cost of both raw materials and processing limit their use to military applications, aircraft, spacecraft, bicycles, medical devices, jewelry, highly stressed components such as connecting rods on expensive sports cars and some premium sports equipment and consumer electronics.

Exam Probability: **Medium**

30. *Answer choices:*

(see index for correct answer)

- a. Gum metal
- b. ATI 425 Titanium Alloy

- c. Titanium Beta C

Guidance: level 1

:: Crystallography ::

The _____ crystal structure is a repeating pattern of 8 atoms that certain materials may adopt as they solidify. While the first known example was diamond, other elements in group 14 also adopt this structure, including a-tin, the semiconductors silicon and germanium, and silicon/germanium alloys in any proportion.

Exam Probability: **High**

31. *Answer choices:*

(see index for correct answer)

- a. Triclinic crystal system
- b. Wurtzite crystal structure
- c. Crystal growth
- d. Trihexagonal tiling

Guidance: level 1

:: Copper alloys ::

_____ is an alloy of copper and zinc, in proportions which can be varied to achieve varying mechanical and electrical properties. It is a substitutional alloy: atoms of the two constituents may replace each other within the same crystal structure. Bronze is an alloy also containing copper, but instead of zinc it has tin.

Exam Probability: **High**

32. *Answer choices:*

(see index for correct answer)

- a. Corinthian bronze
- b. Manganin
- c. Brass
- d. Bell metal

Guidance: level 1

:: Chemical elements ::

_____ is a chemical element with symbol Cr and atomic number 24. It is the first element in group 6. It is a steely-grey, lustrous, hard and brittle transition metal. _____ is also the main additive in stainless steel, to which it adds anti-corrosive properties. _____ is also highly valued as a metal that is able to be highly polished while resisting tarnishing. Polished _____ reflects almost 70% of the visible spectrum, with almost 90% of infrared light being reflected. The name of the element is derived from the Greek word μα, chroma, meaning color, because many _____ compounds are intensely colored.

33. *Answer choices:*

(see index for correct answer)

- a. Chlorine
- b. Rhenium
- c. Nickel
- d. Chromium

Guidance: level 1

:: Polymer chemistry ::

_____ is the relative stereochemistry of adjacent chiral centers within a macromolecule. The practical significance of _____ rests on the effects on the physical properties of the polymer. The regularity of the macromolecular structure influences the degree to which it has rigid, crystalline long range order or flexible, amorphous long range disorder. Precise knowledge of _____ of a polymer also helps understanding at what temperature a polymer melts, how soluble it is in a solvent and its mechanical properties.

34. *Answer choices:*

(see index for correct answer)

- a. Tacticity
- b. Automatic continuous online monitoring of polymerization reactions
- c. Degree of polymerization
- d. Protomer

Guidance: level 1

:: Chemical processes ::

_____ is a chemical process, invented by Charles Goodyear, used to harden rubber. _____ traditionally referred to the treatment of natural rubber with sulfur and this remains the most common example, however the term has also grown to include the hardening of other rubbers via various means. Examples include silicone rubber via room temperature vulcanizing and chloroprene rubber using metal oxides.

Exam Probability: **High**

35. *Answer choices:*

(see index for correct answer)

- a. Char
- b. Kraft process
- c. Derivatization
- d. Vulcanization

Guidance: level 1

:: Liquids ::

_____ is a transparent, tasteless, odorless, and nearly colorless chemical substance, which is the main constituent of Earth's streams, lakes, and oceans, and the fluids of most living organisms. It is vital for all known forms of life, even though it provides no calories or organic nutrients. Its chemical formula is H2O, meaning that each of its molecules contains one oxygen and two hydrogen atoms, connected by covalent bonds. _____ is the name of the liquid state of H2O at standard ambient temperature and pressure. It forms precipitation in the form of rain and aerosols in the form of fog. Clouds are formed from suspended droplets of _____ and ice, its solid state. When finely divided, crystalline ice may precipitate in the form of snow. The gaseous state of _____ is steam or _____ vapor. _____ moves continually through the _____ cycle of evaporation, transpiration , condensation, precipitation, and runoff, usually reaching the sea.

Exam Probability: **Low**

36. *Answer choices:*

(see index for correct answer)

- a. Sodium bifluoride
- b. Water
- c. Float
- d. Macroemulsion

Guidance: level 1

:: Condensed matter physics ::

In physics a _____ is the average velocity attained by charged particles, such as electrons, in a material due to an electric field. In general, an electron in a conductor will propagate randomly at the Fermi velocity, resulting in an average velocity of zero. Applying an electric field adds to this random motion a small net flow in one direction; this is the drift.

Exam Probability: **Low**

37. *Answer choices:*

(see index for correct answer)

- a. Work function
- b. Coercivity
- c. Drift velocity
- d. Slave boson

Guidance: level 1

:: Crystallography ::

A _____ is the interface between two grains, or crystallites, in a polycrystalline material. Grain boundaries are 2D defects in the crystal structure, and tend to decrease the electrical and thermal conductivity of the material. Most grain boundaries are preferred sites for the onset of corrosion and for the precipitation of new phases from the solid. They are also important to many of the mechanisms of creep. On the other hand, grain boundaries disrupt the motion of dislocations through a material, so reducing crystallite size is a common way to improve mechanical strength, as described by the Hall–Petch relationship. The study of grain boundaries and their effects on the mechanical, electrical and other properties of materials forms an important topic in materials science.

Exam Probability: **High**

38. *Answer choices:*

(see index for correct answer)

- a. Bragg plane
- b. Grain boundary
- c. Borrmann effect
- d. Space group

Guidance: level 1

:: Chemical elements ::

_____ is a chemical element with the symbol Zn and atomic number 30. _____ is a slightly brittle metal at room temperature and has a blue-silvery appearance when oxidation is removed. It is the first element in group 12 of the periodic table. In some respects _____ is chemically similar to magnesium: both elements exhibit only one normal oxidation state , and the Zn^{2+} and Mg^{2+} ions are of similar size. _____ is the 24th most abundant element in Earth's crust and has five stable isotopes. The most common _____ ore is sphalerite , a _____ sulfide mineral. The largest workable lodes are in Australia, Asia, and the United States. _____ is refined by froth flotation of the ore, roasting, and final extraction using electricity .

Exam Probability: **Medium**

39. *Answer choices:*

(see index for correct answer)

- a. Zinc
- b. Fluorine
- c. Samarium
- d. Gallium

Guidance: level 1

:: Metal heat treatments ::

_____ is a heat treating process that diffuses nitrogen into the surface of a metal to create a case-hardened surface. These processes are most commonly used on low-carbon, low-alloy steels. They are also used on medium and high-carbon steels, titanium, aluminium and molybdenum. In 2015, _____ was used to generate unique duplex microstructure , known to be associated with strongly enhanced mechanical properties

Exam Probability: **Medium**

40. *Answer choices:*

(see index for correct answer)

- a. Austempering
- b. Cryogenic hardening
- c. Nitriding
- d. Tempering

Guidance: level 1

:: Condensed matter physics ::

The _____ is a concept in quantum mechanics usually referring to the energy difference between the highest and lowest occupied single-particle states in a quantum system of non-interacting fermions at absolute zero temperature.In a Fermi gas, the lowest occupied state is taken to have zero kinetic energy, whereas in a metal, the lowest occupied state is typically taken to mean the bottom of the conduction band.

41. *Answer choices:*

(see index for correct answer)

- • a. Fermi energy
- • b. Metastate
- • c. Constant-energy surface
- • d. Heavy fermion superconductor

Guidance: level 1

:: Microscopy ::

_____ is the technical field of using microscopes to view objects and areas of objects that cannot be seen with the naked eye . There are three well-known branches of _____ : optical, electron, and scanning probe _____ , along with the emerging field of X-ray _____ .

42. *Answer choices:*

(see index for correct answer)

- • a. Telepathology
- • b. Fluorescence interference contrast microscopy
- • c. Microscopy

- d. Digital pathology

Guidance: level 1

:: Polymers ::

A _____ is a large molecule, or macromolecule, composed of many repeated subunits. Due to their broad range of properties, both synthetic and natural _____ s play essential and ubiquitous roles in everyday life. _____ s range from familiar synthetic plastics such as polystyrene to natural bio _____ s such as DNA and proteins that are fundamental to biological structure and function. _____ s, both natural and synthetic, are created via _____ ization of many small molecules, known as monomers. Their consequently large molecular mass relative to small molecule compounds produces unique physical properties, including toughness, viscoelasticity, and a tendency to form glasses and semicrystalline structures rather than crystals. The terms _____ and resin are often synonymous with plastic.

Exam Probability: **Low**

43. *Answer choices:*
(see index for correct answer)

- a. Polyvinyl alcohol
- b. Polyquaternium
- c. Shape-memory polymer
- d. Molecularly imprinted polymer

Guidance: level 1

:: Carbon forms ::

_____ is a chemical element with symbol C and atomic number 6. It is nonmetallic and tetravalent—making four electrons available to form covalent chemical bonds. It belongs to group 14 of the periodic table. Three isotopes occur naturally, 12C and 13C being stable, while 14C is a radionuclide, decaying with a half-life of about 5,730 years. _____ is one of the few elements known since antiquity.

Exam Probability: **High**

44. *Answer choices:*
(see index for correct answer)

- a. Tricarbon
- b. Graphyne
- c. Carbon
- d. Bamboo charcoal

Guidance: level 1

:: Physical chemistry ::

An _____ is a substance that produces an electrically conducting solution when dissolved in a polar solvent, such as water. The dissolved _____ separates into cations and anions, which disperse uniformly through the solvent. Electrically, such a solution is neutral. If an electric potential is applied to such a solution, the cations of the solution are drawn to the electrode that has an abundance of electrons, while the anions are drawn to the electrode that has a deficit of electrons. The movement of anions and cations in opposite directions within the solution amounts to a current. This includes most soluble salts, acids, and bases. Some gases, such as hydrogen chloride, under conditions of high temperature or low pressure can also function as _____ s. _____ solutions can also result from the dissolution of some biological and synthetic polymers , termed "poly _____ s", which contain charged functional groups. A substance that dissociates into ions in solution acquires the capacity to conduct electricity. Sodium, potassium, chloride, calcium, magnesium, and phosphate are examples of _____ s.

Exam Probability: **Low**

45. *Answer choices:*

(see index for correct answer)

- a. Lamellar structure
- b. Dynamic vapor sorption
- c. Reaction dynamics
- d. Electrolyte

Guidance: level 1

:: Plasticizers ::

_____ s or dispersants are additives that increase the plasticity or decrease the viscosity of a material. These are the substances which are added in order to alter their physical properties. These are either liquids with low volatility or solids. They decrease the attraction between polymer chains to make them more flexible. Over the last 60 years more than 30,000 different substances have been evaluated for their plasticizing properties. Of these, only a small number – approximately 50 – are today in commercial use. The dominant applications are for plastics, especially polyvinyl chloride . The properties of other materials may also be modified when blended with _____ s including concrete, clays, and related products. According to 2014 data, the total global market for _____ s was 8.4 million metric tonnes including 1.3 million metric tonnes in Europe.

Exam Probability: **High**

46. *Answer choices:*

(see index for correct answer)

- a. Dioctyl adipate
- b. Dibutyl phthalate
- c. 2,4-Dinitrotoluene
- d. Plasticizer

Guidance: level 1

:: Dielectrics ::

_____ or polyoxybenzylmethylenglycolanhydride was the first plastic made from synthetic components. It is a thermosetting phenol formaldehyde resin, formed from a condensation reaction of phenol with formaldehyde. It was developed by the Belgian-American chemist Leo Baekeland in Yonkers, New York, in 1907.

Exam Probability: **Low**

47. *Answer choices:*

(see index for correct answer)

- a. Bakelite
- b. Dielectric gas
- c. Backstay insulator
- d. Plastic

Guidance: level 1

:: Functional groups ::

_____ s are a class of organic compounds that contain an _____ group—an oxygen atom connected to two alkyl or aryl groups. They have the general formula R–O–R', where R and R' represent the alkyl or aryl groups.

_____ s can again be classified into two varieties: if the alkyl groups are the same on both sides of the oxygen atom, then it is a simple or symmetrical _____ , whereas if they are different, the _____ s are called mixed or unsymmetrical _____ s. A typical example of the first group is the solvent and anesthetic diethyl _____ , commonly referred to simply as " _____ " . _____ s are common in organic chemistry and even more prevalent in biochemistry, as they are common linkages in carbohydrates and lignin.

Exam Probability: **High**

48. *Answer choices:*

- a. Thiolactone
- b. Biuret
- c. Ether
- d. Diol

Guidance: level 1

:: Photonics ::

A _____ is a device that emits light through a process of optical amplification based on the stimulated emission of electromagnetic radiation. The term "_____" originated as an acronym for "Light Amplification by Stimulated Emission of Radiation". The first _____ was built in 1960 by Theodore H. Maiman at Hughes Research Laboratories, based on theoretical work by Charles Hard Townes and Arthur Leonard Schawlow.

Exam Probability: **Medium**

49. *Answer choices:*

(see index for correct answer)

- a. Biophotonics
- b. Transduction
- c. Optical DPSK demodulator
- d. Opticution

Guidance: level 1

:: X-ray scattering ::

_____ , discovered by Arthur Holly Compton, is the scattering of a photon by a charged particle, usually an electron. It results in a decrease in energy of the photon , called the Compton effect. Part of the energy of the photon is transferred to the recoiling electron. Inverse _____ occurs when a charged particle transfers part of its energy to a photon.

Exam Probability: **Medium**

50. *Answer choices:*

(see index for correct answer)

- a. X-ray Raman scattering
- b. Compton scattering
- c. X-ray reflectivity
- d. small angle X-ray scattering

Guidance: level 1

:: Organic chemistry ::

In chemistry, an _____ is generally any chemical compound that contains carbon. Due to carbon's ability to catenate , millions of _____ s are known. Study of the properties and synthesis of _____ s is the discipline known as organic chemistry. For historical reasons, a few classes of carbon-containing compounds , along with a handful of other exceptions , are not classified as _____ s and are considered inorganic. No consensus exists among chemists on precisely which carbon-containing compounds are excluded, making the definition of an _____ elusive.

Exam Probability: **Low**

51. *Answer choices:*

(see index for correct answer)

- a. N-linked glycosylation
- b. Diradical

- c. Aroma compound
- d. Organic compound

Guidance: level 1

:: Metallurgy ::

_____ is a two-phased, lamellar structure composed of alternating layers of ferrite and cementite that occurs in some steels and cast irons. During slow cooling of an iron-carbon alloy, _____ forms by a eutectoid reaction as austenite cools below 727 °C . _____ is a microstructure occurring in many common grades of steels.

Exam Probability: **High**

52. *Answer choices:*
(see index for correct answer)

- a. Refraction
- b. Pearlite
- c. Pyrometallurgy
- d. Moving crack

Guidance: level 1

:: Process chemicals ::

Catalysis is the process of increasing the rate of a chemical reaction by adding a substance known as a _____ , which is not consumed in the catalyzed reaction and can continue to act repeatedly. Because of this, only very small amounts of _____ are required to alter the reaction rate in principle.

Exam Probability: **Low**

53. *Answer choices:*

(see index for correct answer)

- a. Sodium lignosulfonate
- b. Fixation agent
- c. Dispersant
- d. Release agent

Guidance: level 1

:: Crystals ::

_____ s , also dendrons, are branched protoplasmic extensions of a nerve cell that propagate the electrochemical stimulation received from other neural cells to the cell body, or soma, of the neuron from which the _____ s project. Electrical stimulation is transmitted onto _____ s by upstream neurons via synapses which are located at various points throughout the dendritic tree. _____ s play a critical role in integrating these synaptic inputs and in determining the extent to which action potentials are produced by the neuron. Dendritic arborization, also known as dendritic branching, is a multi-step biological process by which neurons form new dendritic trees and branches to create new synapses. The morphology of _____ s such as branch density and grouping patterns are highly correlated to the function of the neuron. Malformation of _____ s is also tightly correlated to impaired nervous system function. Some disorders that are associated with the malformation of _____ s are autism, depression, schizophrenia, Down syndrome and anxiety.

Exam Probability: **High**

54. *Answer choices:*

(see index for correct answer)

- a. Seed crystal
- b. Dendrite
- c. Potassium titanyl phosphate
- d. Hopper crystal

Guidance: level 1

:: Unit operations ::

_____ is a process used to create objects of a fixed cross-sectional profile. A material is pushed through a die of the desired cross-section. The two main advantages of this process over other manufacturing processes are its ability to create very complex cross-sections, and to work materials that are brittle, because the material only encounters compressive and shear stresses. It also forms parts with an excellent surface finish.

Exam Probability: **Low**

55. *Answer choices:*

(see index for correct answer)

- a. Extrusion
- b. DWSIM
- c. Colloid mill
- d. Chemical tank

Guidance: level 1

:: Polymers ::

_____ , commonly abbreviated PET, PETE, or the obsolete PETP or PET-P, is the most common thermoplastic polymer resin of the polyester family and is used in fibres for clothing, containers for liquids and foods, thermoforming for manufacturing, and in combination with glass fibre for engineering resins.

Exam Probability: **High**

56. *Answer choices:*

(see index for correct answer)

- a. Depolymerization
- b. Parylene
- c. Thiomer
- d. Fire-safe polymers

Guidance: level 1

:: Surface chemistry ::

A _____ is an instrument that either measures an angle or allows an object to be rotated to a precise angular position. The term goniometry is derived from two Greek words, gonia, meaning angle, and metron, meaning [[Measurementmeasure].

Exam Probability: **Medium**

57. *Answer choices:*

(see index for correct answer)

- a. Adparticle
- b. Hydrosilylation
- c. Langmuir equation
- d. Goniometer

:: Optical materials ::

_____ s are a group of thermoplastic polymers containing carbonate groups in their chemical structures. _____ s used in engineering are strong, tough materials, and some grades are optically transparent. They are easily worked, molded, and thermoformed. Because of these properties, _____ s find many applications. _____ s do not have a unique resin identification code and are identified as "Other", 7 on the RIC list.

Exam Probability: **Low**

58. *Answer choices:*

(see index for correct answer)

- a. ZBLAN
- b. Germanium
- c. Polycarbonate
- d. Zinc selenide

:: Electron ::

The _____ is a subatomic particle, symbol e or , whose electric charge is negative one elementary charge. _____ s belong to the first generation of the lepton particle family, and are generally thought to be elementary particles because they have no known components or substructure. The _____ has a mass that is approximately 1/1836 that of the proton. Quantum mechanical properties of the _____ include an intrinsic angular momentum of a half-integer value, expressed in units of the reduced Planck constant, h. Being fermions, no two _____ s can occupy the same quantum state, in accordance with the Pauli exclusion principle. Like all elementary particles, _____ s exhibit properties of both particles and waves: they can collide with other particles and can be diffracted like light. The wave properties of _____ s are easier to observe with experiments than those of other particles like neutrons and protons because _____ s have a lower mass and hence a longer de Broglie wavelength for a given energy.

Exam Probability: **High**

59. *Answer choices:*

(see index for correct answer)

- a. Electron rest mass
- b. Electron excitation
- c. Electron
- d. Electron liquid

Guidance: level 1

Analytical chemistry

Analytical chemistry studies and uses instruments and methods used to separate, identify, and quantify matter. In practice, separation, identification or quantification may constitute the entire analysis or be combined with another method. Separation isolates analytes. Qualitative analysis identifies analytes, while quantitative analysis determines the numerical amount or concentration.

:: Analytical chemistry ::

The method of _____ is a type of quantitative analysis approach often used in analytical chemistry whereby the standard is added directly to the aliquots of analyzed sample. This method is used in situations where sample matrix also contributes to the analytical signal, a situation known as the matrix effect, thus making it impossible to compare the analytical signal between sample and standard using the traditional calibration curve approach.

Exam Probability: **Medium**

1. *Answer choices:*

(see index for correct answer)

- a. Standard addition
- b. Detection limit
- c. Colorimetry
- d. Public analyst

Guidance: level 1

:: Analytical chemistry ::

_____ is a processing method for the separation of mixtures of liquids by partial vaporization through a non-porous or porous membrane.

Exam Probability: **Medium**

2. *Answer choices:*

(see index for correct answer)

- a. Lowry protein assay
- b. Elemental analysis
- c. Solid phase extraction
- d. Filter paper

Guidance: level 1

:: Atomic physics ::

In atomic theory and quantum mechanics, an _____ is a mathematical function that describes the wave-like behavior of either one electron or a pair of electrons in an atom. This function can be used to calculate the probability of finding any electron of an atom in any specific region around the atom's nucleus. The term _____ may also refer to the physical region or space where the electron can be calculated to be present, as defined by the particular mathematical form of the orbital.

Exam Probability: **Medium**

3. *Answer choices:*

(see index for correct answer)

- a. Antisymmetric exchange
- b. Atomic orbital
- c. Kaonic hydrogen
- d. Magnetic trap

:: Sodium minerals ::

_____ is a chemical element with symbol Na and atomic number 11. It is a soft, silvery-white, highly reactive metal. _____ is an alkali metal, being in group 1 of the periodic table, because it has a single electron in its outer shell, which it readily donates, creating a positively charged ion—the Na+ cation. Its only stable isotope is 23Na. The free metal does not occur in nature, and must be prepared from compounds. _____ is the sixth most abundant element in the Earth`s crust and exists in numerous minerals such as feldspars, sodalite, and rock salt . Many salts of _____ are highly water-soluble: _____ ions have been leached by the action of water from the Earth`s minerals over eons, and thus _____ and chlorine are the most common dissolved elements by weight in the oceans.

Exam Probability: **Low**

4. *Answer choices:*

(see index for correct answer)

- a. Sodium
- b. Villiaumite
- c. Hydrohalite
- d. Adamsite-

:: Nitrogen hydrides ::

_____ is an inorganic compound with the chemical formula N2H4 , called diamidogen, archaically. It is a simple pnictogen hydride, and is a colorless and flammable liquid with an ammonia-like odour.

Exam Probability: **Medium**

5. *Answer choices:*

(see index for correct answer)

- a. Triazane
- b. Hydrazine
- c. Tetrazene
- d. Hydrazoic acid

Guidance: level 1

:: Electrodes ::

A _____ is an electrode which has a stable and well-known electrode potential. The high stability of the electrode potential is usually reached by employing a redox system with constant concentrations of each participant of the redox reaction.

Exam Probability: **High**

6. *Answer choices:*

(see index for correct answer)

- a. ion-selective electrode
- b. Reference electrode
- c. Liquid metal electrode
- d. Electrode

Guidance: level 1

:: Benzoic acids ::

_____ , $C_7H_6O_2$, is a colorless crystalline solid and a simple aromatic carboxylic acid. The name is derived from gum benzoin, which was for a long time its only known source. _____ occurs naturally in many plants and serves as an intermediate in the biosynthesis of many secondary metabolites. Salts of _____ are used as food preservatives and _____ is an important precursor for the industrial synthesis of many other organic substances. The salts and esters of _____ are known as benzoates .

Exam Probability: **High**

7. *Answer choices:*

(see index for correct answer)

- a. Eprosartan
- b. Mellitic acid
- c. Benzoic acid

- d. Telmisartan

Guidance: level 1

:: Carbohydrates ::

_____ is the generic name for sweet-tasting, soluble carbohydrates, many of which are used in food. The various types of _____ are derived from different sources. Simple _____ s are called monosaccharides and include glucose , fructose, and galactose. "Table _____ " or "granulated _____ " refers to sucrose, a disaccharide of glucose and fructose. In the body, sucrose is hydrolysed into fructose and glucose.

Exam Probability: **Low**

8. *Answer choices:*
(see index for correct answer)

- a. Sugar
- b. Osteonectin
- c. Carbohydrate
- d. Galactose-alpha-1,3-galactose

Guidance: level 1

:: Chemistry ::

In chemistry, a _____ is a material made up of two or more different substances which are mixed. A _____ refers to the physical combination of two or more substances in which the identities are retained and are mixed in the form of solutions, suspensions and colloids.

Exam Probability: **Medium**

9. *Answer choices:*

(see index for correct answer)

- a. Mixture
- b. Magnetic chemistry
- c. Activating agent
- d. Sequence-controlled polymer

Guidance: level 1

:: Solutions ::

_____ is the property of a solid, liquid or gaseous chemical substance called solute to dissolve in a solid, liquid or gaseous solvent. The _____ of a substance fundamentally depends on the physical and chemical properties of the solute and solvent as well as on temperature, pressure and presence of other chemicals of the solution. The extent of the _____ of a substance in a specific solvent is measured as the saturation concentration, where adding more solute does not increase the concentration of the solution and begins to precipitate the excess amount of solute.

10. *Answer choices:*

(see index for correct answer)

- a. Hot water extraction
- b. Desolvation
- c. Condosity
- d. Solubility

Guidance: level 1

:: Analytical chemistry ::

A _____ is a reagent used in chemical analysis which reacts with chemical species that may interfere in the analysis.

11. *Answer choices:*

(see index for correct answer)

- a. Analytical chemistry
- b. Chemoreceptor
- c. Stiff diagram
- d. Masking agent

:: Steroids ::

A _____ is a biologically active organic compound with four rings arranged in a specific molecular configuration. _____ s have two principal biological functions: as important components of cell membranes which alter membrane fluidity; and as signaling molecules. Hundreds of _____ s are found in plants, animals and fungi. All _____ s are manufactured in cells from the sterols lanosterol or cycloartenol . Lanosterol and cycloartenol are derived from the cyclization of the triterpene squalene.

Exam Probability: **High**

12. *Answer choices:*

(see index for correct answer)

- a. Megestrol
- b. Boldione
- c. Gestonorone
- d. Steroid

:: Crystals ::

A _____ or _____ line solid is a solid material whose constituents are arranged in a highly ordered microscopic structure, forming a _____ lattice that extends in all directions. In addition, macroscopic single _____ s are usually identifiable by their geometrical shape, consisting of flat faces with specific, characteristic orientations. The scientific study of _____ s and _____ formation is known as _____ lography. The process of _____ formation via mechanisms of _____ growth is called _____ lization or solidification.

Exam Probability: **Medium**

13. *Answer choices:*

(see index for correct answer)

- a. Mesocrystal
- b. Caesium cadmium chloride
- c. Colloidal crystal
- d. Crystal

Guidance: level 1

:: Cubic minerals ::

_____ is a chemical element with symbol Fe and atomic number 26. It is a metal, that belongs to the first transition series and group 8 of the periodic table. It is by mass the most common element on Earth, forming much of Earth's outer and inner core. It is the fourth most common element in the Earth's crust.

Exam Probability: **High**

14. *Answer choices:*

(see index for correct answer)

- a. Northupite
- b. Iron
- c. Derbyshire Blue John
- d. Hauyne

Guidance: level 1

:: Ketones ::

_____ , or propanone, is the organic compound with the formula 2CO. It is a colorless, volatile, flammable liquid and is the simplest and smallest ketone.

Exam Probability: **Low**

15. *Answer choices:*

(see index for correct answer)

- a. Ionone
- b. Chloroacetone
- c. Nizofenone
- d. Acetone

:: Perturbation theory ::

_____ is the most common tool for approximating the impact of anharmonic terms in the potential energy surface on the vibrational energies.

Exam Probability: **Low**

16. *Answer choices:*

(see index for correct answer)

- a. Perturbation theory
- b. Variational perturbation theory
- c. Eigenvalue perturbation
- d. Method of steepest descent

:: Electrophoresis ::

_____ is a method for separation and analysis of macromolecules and their fragments, based on their size and charge. It is used in clinical chemistry to separate proteins by charge or size and in biochemistry and molecular biology to separate a mixed population of DNA and RNA fragments by length, to estimate the size of DNA and RNA fragments or to separate proteins by charge.

Exam Probability: **High**

17. *Answer choices:*

(see index for correct answer)

- a. Difference gel electrophoresis
- b. Gel electrophoresis
- c. Affinity electrophoresis
- d. Free-flow electrophoresis

Guidance: level 1

:: Gas laws ::

The _____ were developed at the end of the 18th century, when scientists began to realize that relationships between pressure, volume and temperature of a sample of gas could be obtained which would hold to approximation for all gases. Gases behave in a similar way over a wide variety of conditions because they all have molecules which are widely spaced, and the equation of state for an ideal gas is derived from kinetic theory. The earlier _____ are now considered as special cases of the ideal gas equation, with one or more variables held constant.

Exam Probability: **Medium**

18. *Answer choices:*

(see index for correct answer)

- a. Ideal gas law
- b. Van der Waals constants
- c. Gas laws
- d. Acentric factor

Guidance: level 1

:: Carbon forms ::

_____ , archaically referred to as plumbago, is a crystalline form of the element carbon with its atoms arranged in a hexagonal structure. It occurs naturally in this form and is the most stable form of carbon under standard conditions. Under high pressures and temperatures it converts to diamond. _____ is used in pencils and lubricants. Its high conductivity makes it useful in electronic products such as electrodes, batteries, and solar panels.

Exam Probability: **Low**

19. *Answer choices:*

(see index for correct answer)

- a. Nuclear graphite
- b. Exfoliated graphite nano-platelets

- c. Graphite
- d. Graphyne

Guidance: level 1

:: Chemical reactions ::

A _____ is an element or compound that loses an electron to another chemical species in a redox chemical reaction. Since the _____ is losing electrons, it is said to have been oxidized.

Exam Probability: **High**

20. *Answer choices:*

(see index for correct answer)

- a. Lability
- b. Dry media reaction
- c. Reducing agent
- d. Free-radical addition

Guidance: level 1

:: Mass spectrometry ::

_____ or ionisation, is the process by which an atom or a molecule acquires a negative or positive charge by gaining or losing electrons, often in conjunction with other chemical changes. The resulting electrically charged atom or molecule is called an ion. _____ can result from the loss of an electron after collisions with subatomic particles, collisions with other atoms, molecules and ions, or through the interaction with electromagnetic radiation. Heterolytic bond cleavage and heterolytic substitution reactions can result in the formation of ion pairs. _____ can occur through radioactive decay by the internal conversion process, in which an excited nucleus transfers its energy to one of the inner-shell electrons causing it to be ejected.

Exam Probability: **Low**

21. *Answer choices:*

(see index for correct answer)

- a. Ionization
- b. Kratos MS 50
- c. Isotopic labeling
- d. Selected ion monitoring

Guidance: level 1

:: Non-coordinating anions ::

_____ is a polyatomic ion with the molecular formula NO-3 and a molecular mass of 62.0049 u. Organic compounds that contain the _____ ester as a functional group are also called _____ s.

22. *Answer choices:*

(see index for correct answer)

- • a. Bistriflimide
- • b. Tetrachloroaluminate
- • c. Non-coordinating anion
- • d. Tetrafluoroborate

Guidance: level 1

:: Chelating agents ::

_____ s are cyclic chemical compounds that consist of a ring containing several ether groups. The most common _____ s are cyclic oligomers of ethylene oxide, the repeating unit being ethyleneoxy, i.e., –CH2CH2O–. Important members of this series are the tetramer, the pentamer, and the hexamer. The term "crown" refers to the resemblance between the structure of a _____ bound to a cation, and a crown sitting on a person`s head. The first number in a _____ `s name refers to the number of atoms in the cycle, and the second number refers to the number of those atoms that are oxygen. _____ s are much broader than the oligomers of ethylene oxide; an important group are derived from catechol.

23. *Answer choices:*

(see index for correct answer)

- a. Dimercaprol
- b. 1,4,7-Trithiacyclononane
- c. Deferiprone
- d. Crown ether

Guidance: level 1

:: Trigonal minerals ::

_____ is a chemical element with symbol Sb and atomic number 51. A lustrous gray metalloid, it is found in nature mainly as the sulfide mineral stibnite . _____ compounds have been known since ancient times and were powdered for use as medicine and cosmetics, often known by the Arabic name, kohl. Metallic _____ was also known, but it was erroneously identified as lead upon its discovery. The earliest known description of the metal in the West was written in 1540 by Vannoccio Biringuccio.

Exam Probability: **High**

24. *Answer choices:*
(see index for correct answer)

- a. Hematite
- b. Antimony
- c. Delafossite
- d. Beudantite

Guidance: level 1

:: Titration ::

_____ is a technique similar to direct titration of a redox reaction. It is a useful means of characterizing an acid. No indicator is used; instead the potential is measured across the analyte, typically an electrolyte solution. To do this, two electrodes are used, an indicator electrode and a reference electrode. Reference electrodes generally used are hydrogen electrodes, calomel electrodes, and silver chloride electrodes. The indicator electrode forms an electrochemical half cell with the interested ions in the test solution. The reference electrode forms the other half cell.

Exam Probability: **Medium**

25. *Answer choices:*

(see index for correct answer)

- a. Iodometry
- b. Titer
- c. Conductometry
- d. Zeta potential titration

Guidance: level 1

:: Chemical engineering ::

_____ is the net movement of mass from one location, usually meaning stream, phase, fraction or component, to another. _____ occurs in many processes, such as absorption, evaporation, drying, precipitation, membrane filtration, and distillation. _____ is used by different scientific disciplines for different processes and mechanisms. The phrase is commonly used in engineering for physical processes that involve diffusive and convective transport of chemical species within physical systems.

Exam Probability: **Low**

26. *Answer choices:*

(see index for correct answer)

- a. Mass transfer
- b. Steam reforming
- c. Million standard cubic feet per day
- d. Natural-gas processing

Guidance: level 1

:: Charge carriers ::

An ion is an atom or molecule that has a net electrical charge. Since the charge of the electron is equal and opposite to that of the proton , the net charge of an ion is non-zero due to its total number of electrons being unequal to its total number of protons. A _____ is a positively charged ion, with fewer electrons than protons, while an anion is negatively charged, with more electrons than protons. Because of their opposite electric charges, _____ s and anions attract each other and readily form ionic compounds.

27. *Answer choices:*

(see index for correct answer)

- a. Non-radiative life time
- b. Carrier generation and recombination
- c. Ballistic conduction
- d. Velocity overshoot

Guidance: level 1

:: Spectroscopy ::

_____ is the study of the interaction between matter and electromagnetic radiation. Historically, _____ originated through the study of visible light dispersed according to its wavelength, by a prism. Later the concept was expanded greatly to include any interaction with radiative energy as a function of its wavelength or frequency, predominantly in the electromagnetic spectrum, though matter waves and acoustic waves can also be considered forms of radiative energy; recently, with tremendous difficulty, even gravitational waves have been associated with a spectral signature in the context of LIGO and laser interferometry. Spectroscopic data are often represented by an emission spectrum, a plot of the response of interest as a function of wavelength or frequency.

Exam Probability: **Medium**

28. *Answer choices:*

- a. Selection rule
- b. Molecular Hamiltonian
- c. Neutron backscattering
- d. Depolarization ratio

Guidance: level 1

:: Separation processes ::

_____ is the process of separating the components or substances from a liquid mixture by using selective boiling and condensation. _____ may result in essentially complete separation , or it may be a partial separation that increases the concentration of selected components in the mixture. In either case, the process exploits differences in the volatility of the mixture's components. In industrial chemistry, _____ is a unit operation of practically universal importance, but it is a physical separation process, not a chemical reaction.

Exam Probability: **Medium**

29. *Answer choices:*

- a. Precipitation
- b. Decantation
- c. Crystallization of polymers

- d. Distillation

Guidance: level 1

:: Nucleic acids ::

_____ s are the biopolymers, or small biomolecules, essential to all known forms of life. The term _____ is the overall name for DNA and RNA. They are composed of nucleotides, which are the monomers made of three components: a 5-carbon sugar, a phosphate group and a nitrogenous base. If the sugar is a compound ribose, the polymer is RNA ; if the sugar is derived from ribose as deoxyribose, the polymer is DNA .

Exam Probability: **Low**

30. *Answer choices:*
(see index for correct answer)

- a. Nucleic acid
- b. Genomic signature
- c. Aptamer
- d. Nucleic acid analogue

Guidance: level 1

:: Scattering ::

Scattering is a general physical process where some forms of radiation, such as light, sound, or moving particles, are forced to deviate from a straight trajectory by one or more paths due to localized non-uniformities in the medium through which they pass. In conventional use, this also includes deviation of reflected radiation from the angle predicted by the law of reflection. Reflections that undergo scattering are often called diffuse reflections and unscattered reflections are called specular reflections.

Exam Probability: **Low**

31. *Answer choices:*

(see index for correct answer)

- a. Light scattering
- b. Discrete dipole approximation
- c. Inelastic collision
- d. Chaotic scattering

Guidance: level 1

:: Minerals ::

A _____ is, broadly speaking, a solid chemical compound that occurs naturally in pure form. A rock may consist of a single _____ , or may be an aggregate of two or more different _____ s, spacially segregated into distinct phases. Compounds that occur only in living beings are usually excluded, but some _____ s are often biogenic and/or are organic compounds in the sense of chemistry . Moreover, living beings often synthesize inorganic _____ s that also occur in rocks.

32. *Answer choices:*

(see index for correct answer)

- a. Peak minerals
- b. Mineral
- c. Layered double hydroxides
- d. Sascab

Guidance: level 1

:: Functional groups ::

In organic chemistry, a _____ group is a functional group composed of a carbon atom double-bonded to an oxygen atom: C=O. It is common to several classes of organic compounds, as part of many larger functional groups. A compound containing a _____ group is often referred to as a _____ compound.

33. *Answer choices:*

(see index for correct answer)

- a. Epoxide
- b. Nitrate ester

- c. Carbonyl
- d. Silyl ether

Guidance: level 1

:: Ion source ::

_____ is a soft ionization technique used in mass spectrometry. This was first introduced by Burnaby Munson and Frank H. Field in 1966. This technique is a branch of gaseous ion-molecule chemistry. Reagent gas molecules are ionized by electron ionization, which subsequently react with analyte molecules in the gas phase in order to achieve ionization. Negative _____ , charge-exchange _____ and atmospheric-pressure _____ are some of the common variations of this technique. CI has several important applications in identification, structure elucidation and quantitation of organic compounds. Beside the applications in analytical chemistry, the usefulness in _____ extends toward biochemical, biological and medicinal fields as well.

Exam Probability: **High**

34. *Answer choices:*

(see index for correct answer)

- a. Electron capture ionization
- b. Laser spray ionization
- c. Chemical ionization
- d. Extractive electrospray ionization

Guidance: level 1

:: Functional groups ::

_____ s are a class of organic compounds that contain an _____ group—an oxygen atom connected to two alkyl or aryl groups. They have the general formula R–O–R', where R and R' represent the alkyl or aryl groups. _____ s can again be classified into two varieties: if the alkyl groups are the same on both sides of the oxygen atom, then it is a simple or symmetrical _____ , whereas if they are different, the _____ s are called mixed or unsymmetrical _____ s. A typical example of the first group is the solvent and anesthetic diethyl _____ , commonly referred to simply as " _____ ". _____ s are common in organic chemistry and even more prevalent in biochemistry, as they are common linkages in carbohydrates and lignin.

Exam Probability: **Low**

35. *Answer choices:*

(see index for correct answer)

- a. Alcohol
- b. Nitronium ion
- c. Ether
- d. Thioacetal

Guidance: level 1

:: Coordination chemistry ::

The _____ , sometimes referred to as oxidation number, describes the degree of oxidation of an atom in a chemical compound. Conceptually, the _____ , which may be positive, negative or zero, is the hypothetical charge that an atom would have if all bonds to atoms of different elements were 100% ionic, with no covalent component. This is never exactly true for real bonds.

Exam Probability: **High**

36. *Answer choices:*

(see index for correct answer)

- a. Coordination number
- b. Chinese lantern structure
- c. Associative substitution
- d. Hapticity

Guidance: level 1

:: Analytical chemistry ::

In analytical chemistry, the _____ , lower limit of detection, or LOD , is the lowest quantity of a substance that can be distinguished from the absence of that substance with a stated confidence level . The _____ is estimated from the mean of the blank, the standard deviation of the blank and some confidence factor. Another consideration that affects the _____ is the accuracy of the model used to predict concentration from the raw analytical signal.

37. *Answer choices:*

(see index for correct answer)

- a. Secretion assay
- b. Loss on ignition
- c. Detection limit
- d. Chemical equilibrium

Guidance: level 1

:: Cations ::

The _____ cation is a positively charged polyatomic ion with the chemical formula $NH+4$. It is formed by the protonation of ammonia . _____ is also a general name for positively charged or protonated substituted amines and quaternary _____ cations , where one or more hydrogen atoms are replaced by organic groups .

Exam Probability: **Low**

38. *Answer choices:*

(see index for correct answer)

- a. Kryptonium ion
- b. Oxalyl

- c. Ammonium
- d. Xenonium

Guidance: level 1

:: Titration ::

_____ , also known as titrimetry, is a common laboratory method of quantitative chemical analysis that is used to determine the concentration of an identified analyte. Since volume measurements play a key role in _____ , it is also known as volumetric analysis. A reagent, called the titrant or titrator is prepared as a standard solution. A known concentration and volume of titrant reacts with a solution of analyte or titrand to determine concentration. The volume of titrant reacted is called _____ volume.

Exam Probability: **Medium**

39. *Answer choices:*

(see index for correct answer)

- a. Iodometry
- b. titrant
- c. Titer
- d. Titration

Guidance: level 1

:: Membrane technology ::

A _____ is a selective barrier; it allows some things to pass through but stops others. Such things may be molecules, ions, or other small particles. Biological _____ s include cell _____ s ; nuclear _____ s, which cover a cell nucleus; and tissue _____ s, such as mucosae and serosae. Synthetic _____ s are made by humans for use in laboratories and industry .

Exam Probability: **Medium**

40. *Answer choices:*

(see index for correct answer)

- a. Membrane
- b. Reverse osmosis
- c. Gaseous diffusion
- d. Thin-film composite membrane

Guidance: level 1

:: Oxoanions ::

In chemistry, a _____ is a salt of carbonic acid , characterized by the presence of the _____ ion, a polyatomic ion with the formula of $CO2-3$. The name may also refer to a _____ ester, an organic compound containing the _____ group C2.

41. *Answer choices:*

(see index for correct answer)

- a. Hypochlorite
- b. Antimonate
- c. Periodate
- d. Carbonate

Guidance: level 1

:: Functional groups ::

In chemistry, an _____ is a chemical compound derived from an acid in which at least one –OH group is replaced by an –O–alkyl group. Usually, _____ s are derived from a carboxylic acid and an alcohol. Glycerides, which are fatty acid _____ s of glycerol, are important _____ s in biology, being one of the main classes of lipids, and making up the bulk of animal fats and vegetable oils. _____ s with low molecular weight are commonly used as fragrances and found in essential oils and pheromones. Phospho _____ s form the backbone of DNA molecules. Nitrate _____ s, such as nitroglycerin, are known for their explosive properties, while poly _____ s are important plastics, with monomers linked by _____ moieties. _____ s usually have a sweet smell and are considered high-quality solvents for a broad array of plastics, plasticizers, resins, and lacquers. They are also one of the largest classes of synthetic lubricants on the commercial market.

42. *Answer choices:*

(see index for correct answer)

- a. Episulfide
- b. Carbazide
- c. Ester
- d. Nitrate ester

Guidance: level 1

:: Chemical elements ::

_____ is a chemical element with symbol I and atomic number 53. The heaviest of the stable halogens, it exists as a lustrous, purple-black non-metallic solid at standard conditions that melts to form a deep violet liquid at 114 degrees Celsius, and boils to a violet gas at 184 degrees Celsius. The element was discovered by the French chemist Bernard Courtois in 1811. It was named two years later by Joseph Louis Gay-Lussac from this property, after the Greek d "violet-coloured".

Exam Probability: **High**

43. *Answer choices:*

(see index for correct answer)

- a. Ununseptium
- b. Lanthanum
- c. Curium

- d. Iodine

Guidance: level 1

:: Chromatography ::

_____ includes any chromatographic method that uses a hydrophobic stationary phase. RPC refers to liquid chromatography.

Exam Probability: **Medium**

44. *Answer choices:*
(see index for correct answer)

- a. Reversed-phase chromatography
- b. Displacement chromatography
- c. Countercurrent chromatography
- d. History of chromatography

Guidance: level 1

:: Chemical properties ::

Molar concentration is a measure of the concentration of a chemical species, in particular of a solute in a solution, in terms of amount of substance per unit volume of solution. In chemistry, the most commonly used unit for _____ is the number of moles per litre, having the unit symbol mol/L. A solution with a concentration of 1 mol/L is said to be 1 molar, commonly designated as 1 M.

Exam Probability: **Medium**

45. *Answer choices:*

(see index for correct answer)

- a. Molarity
- b. metastability
- c. miscibility
- d. miscible

Guidance: level 1

:: Spectroscopy ::

_____ is the study of the electromagnetic radiation absorbed and emitted by atoms. Since unique elements have characteristic spectra, _____ , specifically the electromagnetic spectrum or mass spectrum, is applied for determination of elemental compositions. It can be divided by atomization source or by the type of spectroscopy used. In the latter case, the main division is between optical and mass spectrometry. Mass spectrometry generally gives significantly better analytical performance, but is also significantly more complex. This complexity translates into higher purchase costs, higher operational costs, more operator training, and a greater number of components that can potentially fail. Because optical spectroscopy is often less expensive and has performance adequate for many tasks, it is far more common Atomic absorption spectrometers are one of the most commonly sold and used analytical devices.

Exam Probability: **Low**

46. *Answer choices:*

(see index for correct answer)

- a. Immobilized enzyme ESR
- b. Jablonski diagram
- c. Absorption band
- d. The Unscrambler

Guidance: level 1

:: Functional analysis ::

An _____ is a type of eigenvector that is both a unique characteristic of a parameter and a function. Like eigenvectors, the function's direction remains the same when a linear transformation is applied and instead it is only multiplied by a scaling factor . For example, if you imagine resizing a picture, _____ s are the unmoving axes along which the linear transformation stretches, compresses or flips the data. In multi-dimensional data analysis, using a function in place of a simple eigenvector allows you to model all the dimensions of any given space in one formula.

Exam Probability: **Medium**

47. *Answer choices:*

(see index for correct answer)

- a. commutative
- b. orthonormal
- c. Eigenfunction

Guidance: level 1

:: Chemical elements ::

_____ is a chemical element with symbol Ce and atomic number 58. _____ is a soft, ductile and silvery-white metal that tarnishes when exposed to air, and it is soft enough to be cut with a knife. _____ is the second element in the lanthanide series, and while it often shows the +3 oxidation state characteristic of the series, it also exceptionally has a stable +4 state that does not oxidize water. It is also considered one of the rare-earth elements. _____ has no biological role and is not very toxic.

48. *Answer choices:*

(see index for correct answer)

- a. Gadolinium
- b. Cerium
- c. Dubnium
- d. Americium

Guidance: level 1

:: Electrolysis ::

In chemistry and manufacturing, _____ is a technique that uses a direct electric current to drive an otherwise non-spontaneous chemical reaction. _____ is commercially important as a stage in the separation of elements from naturally occurring sources such as ores using an electrolytic cell. The voltage that is needed for _____ to occur is called the decomposition potential.

Exam Probability: **High**

49. *Answer choices:*

(see index for correct answer)

- a. High-temperature electrolysis
- b. Alkaline water electrolysis

- c. Betts electrolytic process
- d. Hydrion

Guidance: level 1

:: Electrodes ::

The _____ , is a redox electrode which forms the basis of the thermodynamic scale of oxidation-reduction potentials. Its absolute electrode potential is estimated to be 4.44 ± 0.02 V at 25 °C, but to form a basis for comparison with all other electrode reactions, hydrogen's standard electrode potential is declared to be zero volts only at 298K. Potentials of any other electrodes are compared with that of the _____ at the same temperature.

Exam Probability: **Medium**

50. *Answer choices:*

(see index for correct answer)

- a. Electrode
- b. Standard hydrogen electrode
- c. Liquid metal electrode
- d. Fluoride selective electrode

Guidance: level 1

:: Chemical engineering ::

_____ or equilibrium _____ is defined as the pressure exerted by a vapor in thermodynamic equilibrium with its condensed phases at a given temperature in a closed system. The equilibrium _____ is an indication of a liquid's evaporation rate. It relates to the tendency of particles to escape from the liquid . A substance with a high _____ at normal temperatures is often referred to as volatile. The pressure exhibited by vapor present above a liquid surface is known as _____ . As the temperature of a liquid increases, the kinetic energy of its molecules also increases. As the kinetic energy of the molecules increases, the number of molecules transitioning into a vapor also increases, thereby increasing the _____ .

Exam Probability: **High**

51. *Answer choices:*

(see index for correct answer)

- a. True vapor pressure
- b. Supercritical steam generator
- c. Dialysis tubing
- d. Solid-state reaction route

Guidance: level 1

:: Chromatography ::

_____ is a family of electrokinetic separation methods performed in submillimeter diameter capillaries and in micro- and nanofluidic channels. Very often, CE refers to capillary zone electrophoresis , but other electrophoretic techniques including capillary gel electrophoresis , capillary isoelectric focusing , capillary isotachophoresis and micellar electrokinetic chromatography belong also to this class of methods. In CE methods, analytes migrate through electrolyte solutions under the influence of an electric field. Analytes can be separated according to ionic mobility and/or partitioning into an alternate phase via non-covalent interactions. Additionally, analytes may be concentrated or "focused" by means of gradients in conductivity and pH.

Exam Probability: **High**

52. *Answer choices:*
(see index for correct answer)

- a. Rodrigues equation
- b. Van Deemter equation
- c. Displacement chromatography
- d. Retardation factor

Guidance: level 1

:: Colloidal chemistry ::

A _____ or micella is an aggregate of surfactant molecules dispersed in a liquid colloid. A typical _____ in aqueous solution forms an aggregate with the hydrophilic "head" regions in contact with surrounding solvent, sequestering the hydrophobic single-tail regions in the _____ centre. This phase is caused by the packing behavior of single-tail lipids in a bilayer. The difficulty filling all the volume of the interior of a bilayer, while accommodating the area per head group forced on the molecule by the hydration of the lipid head group, leads to the formation of the _____ . This type of _____ is known as a normal-phase _____ . Inverse _____ s have the head groups at the centre with the tails extending out . _____ s are approximately spherical in shape. Other phases, including shapes such as ellipsoids, cylinders, and bilayers, are also possible. The shape and size of a _____ are a function of the molecular geometry of its surfactant molecules and solution conditions such as surfactant concentration, temperature, pH, and ionic strength. The process of forming _____ s is known as micellisation and forms part of the phase behaviour of many lipids according to their polymorphism.

Exam Probability: **Medium**

53. *Answer choices:*

(see index for correct answer)

- a. Critical micelle concentration
- b. Micelle
- c. Relative permittivity
- d. Turbidity

Guidance: level 1

:: Radiation ::

Absorption spectroscopy refers to spectroscopic techniques that measure the absorption of radiation, as a function of frequency or wavelength, due to its interaction with a sample. The sample absorbs energy, i.e., photons, from the radiating field. The intensity of the absorption varies as a function of frequency, and this variation is the _____ . Absorption spectroscopy is performed across the electromagnetic spectrum.

Exam Probability: **Low**

54. *Answer choices:*

(see index for correct answer)

- a. Absorption spectrum
- b. Cosmic ray
- c. Radio Research Laboratory
- d. Absorption edge

Guidance: level 1

:: Chromatography ::

_____ is a method of separating biochemical mixture based on a highly specific interaction between antigen and antibody, enzyme and substrate, receptor and ligand, or protein and nucleic acid. It is a type of chromatographic laboratory technique used for purifying biological molecules within a mixture by exploiting molecular properties.

Exam Probability: **High**

55. *Answer choices:*

(see index for correct answer)

- a. Purnell equation
- b. Distribution constant
- c. Reversed-phase chromatography
- d. Chromatographic response function

Guidance: level 1

:: Infrared spectroscopy ::

_____ involves the interaction of infrared radiation with matter. It covers a range of techniques, mostly based on absorption spectroscopy. As with all spectroscopic techniques, it can be used to identify and study chemicals. Samples may be solid, liquid, or gas. The method or technique of _____ is conducted with an instrument called an infrared spectrometer to produce an infrared spectrum. An IR spectrum can be visualized in a graph of infrared light absorbance on the vertical axis vs. frequency or wavelength on the horizontal axis. Typical units of frequency used in IR spectra are reciprocal centimeters, with the symbol cm-1. Units of IR wavelength are commonly given in micrometers, symbol μm, which are related to wave numbers in a reciprocal way. A common laboratory instrument that uses this technique is a Fourier transform infrared spectrometer. Two-dimensional IR is also possible as discussed below.

Exam Probability: **High**

56. *Answer choices:*

(see index for correct answer)

- a. Diffuse reflectance infrared fourier transform
- b. Hagen-Rubens relation
- c. Hyperspectral imaging
- d. Two-dimensional infrared spectroscopy

Guidance: level 1

:: Titration ::

An _____ is an investigative procedure in laboratory medicine, pharmacology, environmental biology and molecular biology for qualitatively assessing or quantitatively measuring the presence, amount, or functional activity of a target entity . The analyte can be a drug, a biochemical substance, or a cell in an organism or organic sample. The measured entity is generally called the analyte, the measurand or the target of the _____ . The _____ usually aims to measure an intensive property of the analyte and express it in the relevant measurement unit .

Exam Probability: **Low**

57. *Answer choices:*

(see index for correct answer)

- a. Iodometry
- b. Titer
- c. Kjeldahl method
- d. Nonaqueous titration

:: Organic acids ::

An _____ is an organic compound with acidic properties. The most common _____ s are the carboxylic acids, whose acidity is associated with their carboxyl group –COOH. Sulfonic acids, containing the group –SO2OH, are relatively stronger acids. Alcohols, with –OH, can act as acids but they are usually very weak. The relative stability of the conjugate base of the acid determines its acidity. Other groups can also confer acidity, usually weakly: the thiol group –SH, the enol group, and the phenol group. In biological systems, organic compounds containing these groups are generally referred to as _____ s.

Exam Probability: **Low**

58. *Answer choices:*

(see index for correct answer)

- a. Organic acid
- b. Teichoic acid
- c. Uric acid
- d. Polyelectrolyte

:: Starch ::

_____ is a simple sugar with the molecular formula C6H12O6. _____ is the most abundant monosaccharide, a subcategory of carbohydrates. _____ is mainly made by plants and most algae during photosynthesis from water and carbon dioxide, using energy from sunlight. There it is used to make cellulose in cell walls, which is the most abundant carbohydrate. In energy metabolism, _____ is the most important source of energy in all organisms. _____ for metabolism is partially stored as a polymer, in plants mainly as starch and amylopectin and in animals as glycogen. _____ circulates in the blood of animals as blood sugar. The naturally occurring form of _____ is - _____ , while - _____ is produced synthetically in comparatively small amounts and is of lesser importance.

Exam Probability: **Low**

59. *Answer choices:*

(see index for correct answer)

- a. Corn syrup
- b. Retrogradation
- c. Dialdehyde starch
- d. Waxy corn

Guidance: level 1

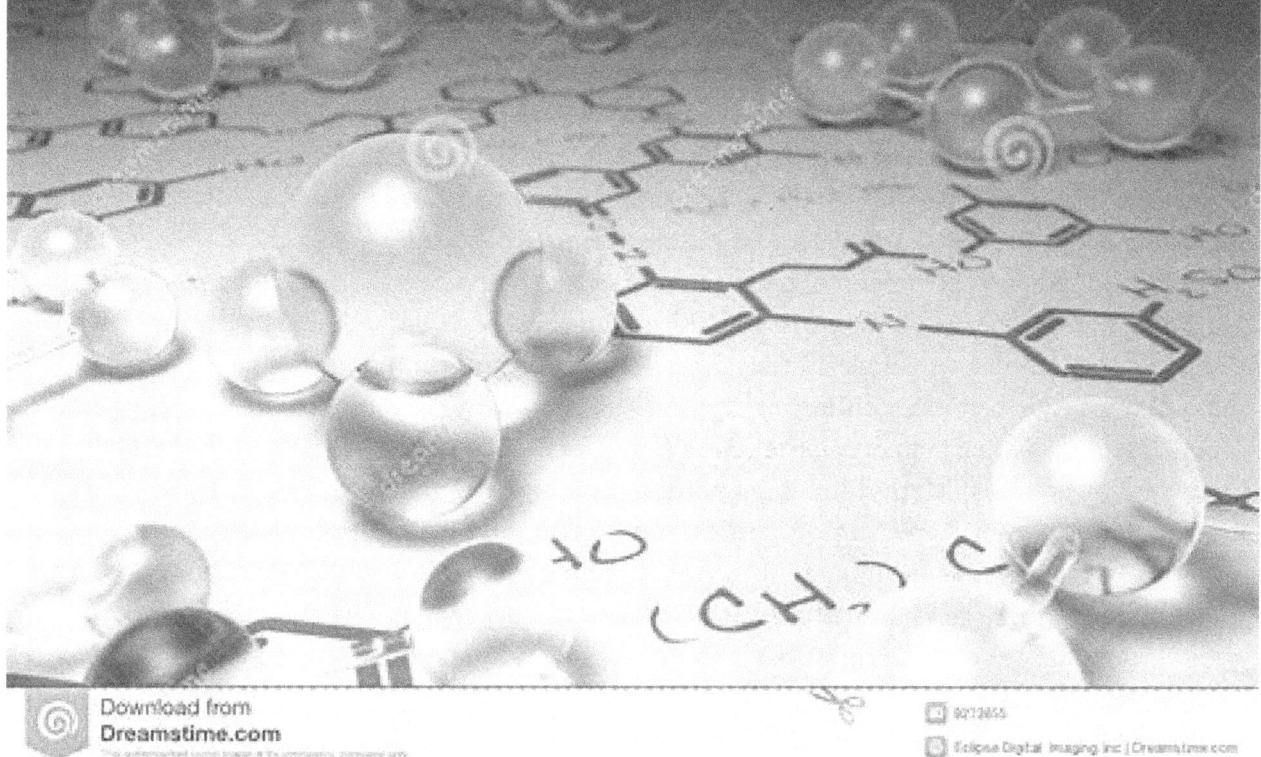

Organic chemistry

Organic chemistry is the chemistry subdiscipline for the scientific study of structure, properties, and reactions of organic compounds and organic materials (materials that contain carbon atoms). Study of structure determines their chemical composition and formula. Study of properties includes physical and chemical properties, and evaluation of chemical reactivity to understand their behavior. The study of organic reactions includes the chemical synthesis of natural products, drugs, and polymers, and study of individual organic molecules in the laboratory and via theoretical study.

:: Halogenated solvents ::

The haloalkanes are a group of chemical compounds derived from alkanes containing one or more halogens. They are a subset of the general class of halocarbons, although the distinction is not often made. Haloalkanes are widely used commercially and, consequently, are known under many chemical and commercial names. They are used as flame retardants, fire extinguishants, refrigerants, propellants, solvents, and pharmaceuticals. Subsequent to the widespread use in commerce, many halocarbons have also been shown to be serious pollutants and toxins. For example, the chlorofluorocarbons have been shown to lead to ozone depletion. Methyl bromide is a controversial fumigant. Only haloalkanes which contain chlorine, bromine, and iodine are a threat to the ozone layer, but fluorinated volatile haloalkanes in theory may have activity as greenhouse gases. Methyl iodide, a naturally occurring substance, however, does not have ozone-depleting properties and the United States Environmental Protection Agency has designated the compound a non-ozone layer depleter. For more information, see Halomethane. Haloalkane or _____ are the compounds which have the general formula "RX" where R is an alkyl or substituted alkyl group and X is a halogen .

Exam Probability: **High**

1. *Answer choices:*

(see index for correct answer)

- a. Chlorobenzene
- b. Parachlorobenzotrifluoride
- c. Alkyl halides
- d. 1,1,1,2-Tetrachloroethane

Guidance: level 1

:: Chelating agents ::

_____ is a weak organic acid that has the chemical formula C6H8O7. It occurs naturally in citrus fruits. In biochemistry, it is an intermediate in the _____ cycle, which occurs in the metabolism of all aerobic organisms.

Exam Probability: **Medium**

2. *Answer choices:*

(see index for correct answer)

- a. Chelex 100
- b. Citric acid
- c. 2,3-Dihydroxybenzoic acid
- d. 1,4,7-Triazacyclononane

Guidance: level 1

:: Salts ::

A _____ is a binary phase, of which one part is a halogen atom and the other part is an element or radical that is less electronegative than the halogen, to make a fluoride, chloride, bromide, iodide, astatide, or theoretically tennesside compound. The alkali metals combine directly with halogens under appropriate conditions forming _____ s of the general formula, MX . Many salts are _____ s; the hal- syllable in _____ and halite reflects this correlation. All Group 1 metals form _____ s that are white solids at room temperature.

Exam Probability: **Medium**

3. *Answer choices:*

(see index for correct answer)

- a. Pyridinium p-toluenesulfonate
- b. Bicarbonate
- c. Dead Sea salt
- d. Halide

Guidance: level 1

:: Acids ::

_____ is a chemical compound with the chemical formula H_2CO_3 . It is also a name sometimes given to solutions of carbon dioxide in water , because such solutions contain small amounts of H_2CO_3. In physiology, _____ is described as volatile acid or respiratory acid, because it is the only acid excreted as a gas by the lungs. It plays an important role in the bicarbonate buffer system to maintain acid–base homeostasis.

Exam Probability: **Medium**

4. *Answer choices:*

(see index for correct answer)

- a. Sulfur oxoacid
- b. Gastric acid
- c. Thiocyanic acid
- d. Hydronium

Guidance: level 1

:: Alkylbenzenes ::

_________ , also known as toluol , is an aromatic hydrocarbon. It is a colorless, water-insoluble liquid with the smell associated with paint thinners. It is a mono-substituted benzene derivative, consisting of a CH3 group attached to a phenyl group. As such, its IUPAC systematic name is methylbenzene. _________ is predominantly used as an industrial feedstock and a solvent.

Exam Probability: **High**

5. *Answer choices:*

(see index for correct answer)

- a. Toluene
- b. P-Cymene
- c. O-Xylene
- d. Tetramethylbenzenes

Guidance: level 1

:: Aromatic bases ::

_____ is a basic heterocyclic organic compound with the chemical formula C5H5N. It is structurally related to benzene, with one methine group replaced by a nitrogen atom. It is a highly flammable, weakly alkaline, water-soluble liquid with a distinctive, unpleasant fish-like smell. _____ is colorless, but older or impure samples can appear yellow. The _____ ring occurs in many important compounds, including agrochemicals, pharmaceuticals, and vitamins. Historically, _____ was produced from coal tar. Today it is synthesized on the scale of about 20,000 tonnes per year worldwide.

Exam Probability: **High**

6. *Answer choices:*

(see index for correct answer)

- a. Cinnoline
- b. Benzoxazole
- c. Pyridine
- d. Pyrimidine

Guidance: level 1

:: Functional groups ::

The _____ , NO+2, is a cation. It is an onium ion because of its tetravalent nitrogen atom and +1 charge, similar in that regard to ammonium. It is created by the removal of an electron from the paramagnetic nitrogen dioxide molecule, or the protonation of nitric acid .

7. *Answer choices:*

(see index for correct answer)

- a. Schiff base
- b. Carbonyl
- c. Nitronium ion
- d. Urea

Guidance: level 1

:: Molecular geometry ::

In molecular geometry, _____ or bond distance is the average distance between nuclei of two bonded atoms in a molecule. It is a transferable property of a bond between atoms of fixed types, relatively independent of the rest of the molecule.

Exam Probability: **Low**

8. *Answer choices:*

(see index for correct answer)

- a. RNA CoSSMos
- b. Bond length
- c. Cyclic compound

- d. Tricapped trigonal prismatic molecular geometry

Guidance: level 1

:: Sodium minerals ::

_____ is a mineral composed primarily of sodium chloride , a chemical compound belonging to the larger class of _____ s; _____ in its natural form as a crystalline mineral is known as rock _____ or halite. _____ is present in vast quantities in seawater, where it is the main mineral constituent. The open ocean has about 35 grams of solids per liter of sea water, a salinity of 3.5%.

Exam Probability: **Low**

9. *Answer choices:*
(see index for correct answer)

- a. Clarkeite
- b. Salt
- c. Eudialyte group
- d. Nitratine

Guidance: level 1

:: Physical quantities ::

A _____ is any property that is measurable, whose value describes a state of a physical system. The changes in the physical properties of a system can be used to describe its changes between momentary states. Physical properties are often referred to as observables. They are not modal properties. Quantifiable _____ is called physical quantity.

Exam Probability: **Medium**

10. *Answer choices:*

(see index for correct answer)

- a. Physical property
- b. voltage
- c. Physical properties
- d. potential difference

Guidance: level 1

:: Physical chemistry ::

In chemistry, a _____ is an abstract one-dimensional coordinate which represents progress along a reaction pathway. It is usually a geometric parameter that changes during the conversion of one or more molecular entities. In molecular dynamics simulations, a _____ is called collective variable.

Exam Probability: **High**

11. *Answer choices:*

(see index for correct answer)

- a. Van der Waals surface
- b. Random coil
- c. Reaction coordinate
- d. Radial distribution function

Guidance: level 1

:: Functional groups ::

In chemistry, a _____ is an organic compound with the structure RCR`, where R and R` can be a variety of carbon-containing substituents. _____ s and aldehydes are simple compounds that contain a carbonyl group . They are considered "simple" because they do not have reactive groups like -OH or -Cl attached directly to the carbon atom in the carbonyl group, as in carboxylic acids containing -COOH. Many _____ s are known and many are of great importance in industry and in biology. Examples include many sugars and the industrial solvent acetone, which is the smallest _____ .

Exam Probability: **Low**

12. *Answer choices:*

(see index for correct answer)

- a. Semicarbazide
- b. Semicarbazone

- c. Cyanate ester
- d. Urea

Guidance: level 1

:: Physical chemistry ::

In chemistry, a _____ is a special type of homogeneous mixture composed of two or more substances. In such a mixture, a solute is a substance dissolved in another substance, known as a solvent. The mixing process of a _____ happens at a scale where the effects of chemical polarity are involved, resulting in interactions that are specific to solvation. The _____ assumes the phase of the solvent when the solvent is the larger fraction of the mixture, as is commonly the case. The concentration of a solute in a _____ is the mass of that solute expressed as a percentage of the mass of the whole _____ . The term aqueous _____ is when one of the solvents is water.

Exam Probability: **Medium**

13. *Answer choices:*

(see index for correct answer)

- a. ISO 31-8
- b. Solution
- c. Van der Waals surface
- d. Chemical potential

Guidance: level 1

:: Neurosteroids ::

_____ is an endogenous steroid and progestogen sex hormone involved in the menstrual cycle, pregnancy, and embryogenesis of humans and other species. It belongs to a group of steroid hormones called the progestogens, and is the major progestogen in the body. _____ has a variety of important functions in the body. It is also a crucial metabolic intermediate in the production of other endogenous steroids, including the sex hormones and the corticosteroids, and plays an important role in brain function as a neurosteroid.

Exam Probability: **Low**

14. *Answer choices:*

(see index for correct answer)

- a. Pregnenolone
- b. Neuroactive steroid
- c. Pregnane
- d. Tetrahydrodeoxycorticosterone

Guidance: level 1

:: Cycloalkanes ::

_____ is a highly flammable alicyclic hydrocarbon with chemical formula C_5H_{10} and CAS number 287-92-3, consisting of a ring of five carbon atoms each bonded with two hydrogen atoms above and below the plane. It occurs as a colorless liquid with a petrol-like odor. Its melting point is -94 °C and its boiling point is 49 °C. _____ is in the class of cycloalkanes, being alkanes that have one or more rings of carbon atoms. It is formed by cracking cyclohexane in the presence of alumina at a high temperature and pressure.

Exam Probability: **High**

15. *Answer choices:*

(see index for correct answer)

- a. Cycloundecane
- b. Cyclotetradecane
- c. Basketane
- d. Cyclopentane

Guidance: level 1

:: Anions ::

_____ s are a group of compounds with the structure R-O-O-R. The O-O group in a _____ is called the _____ group or peroxo group. In contrast to oxide ions, the oxygen atoms in the _____ ion have an oxidation state of -1.

Exam Probability: **Medium**

16. *Answer choices:*

(see index for correct answer)

- a. Selenide
- b. Hydride
- c. Peroxide
- d. Hydrogen anion

Guidance: level 1

:: Carbohydrates ::

_____ is the metabolic pathway that converts glucose $C_6H_{12}O_6$, into pyruvate, $CH_3COCOO^- + H^+$. The free energy released in this process is used to form the high-energy molecules ATP and NADH . _____ is a sequence of ten enzyme-catalyzed reactions. Most monosaccharides, such as fructose and galactose, can be converted to one of these intermediates. The intermediates may also be directly useful. For example, the intermediate dihydroxyacetone phosphate is a source of the glycerol that combines with fatty acids to form fat.

Exam Probability: **Medium**

17. *Answer choices:*

(see index for correct answer)

- a. Amylopectin
- b. Glycogen synthase

- c. Glycolysis
- d. Isomaltooligosaccharide

Guidance: level 1

:: Carbohydrate chemistry ::

In chemistry, a _____ is a molecule in which a sugar is bound to another functional group via a glycosidic bond. _____ s play numerous important roles in living organisms. Many plants store chemicals in the form of inactive _____ s. These can be activated by enzyme hydrolysis, which causes the sugar part to be broken off, making the chemical available for use. Many such plant _____ s are used as medications. Several species of Heliconius butterfly are capable of incorporating these plant compounds as a form of chemical defense against predators. In animals and humans, poisons are often bound to sugar molecules as part of their elimination from the body.

Exam Probability: **Medium**

18. *Answer choices:*

(see index for correct answer)

- a. Polysaccharide
- b. Reducing sugar
- c. Glycoprotein
- d. Sophorolipid

Guidance: level 1

:: Condensation reactions ::

An _____ is a condensation reaction in organic chemistry in which an enol or an enolate ion reacts with a carbonyl compound to form a ß-hydroxyaldehyde or ß-hydroxyketone , followed by dehydration to give a conjugated enone.

Exam Probability: **Medium**

19. *Answer choices:*

(see index for correct answer)

- a. Benzoin condensation
- b. Aldol condensation
- c. Self-condensation

Guidance: level 1

:: Isomerism ::

_____ s are a type of a stereoisomer. Diasteoreomers are defined as non-mirror image non-identical stereoisomers. Hence, they occur when two or more stereoisomers of a compound have different configurations at one or more of the equivalent stereocenters and are not mirror images of each other. When two diastereoisomers differ from each other at only one stereocenter they are epimers. Each stereocenter gives rise to two different configurations and thus typically increases the number of stereoisomers by a factor of two.

20. *Answer choices:*

(see index for correct answer)

- a. Isomer
- b. Isotopomers
- c. Electromerism
- d. Diastereomer

Guidance: level 1

:: Equilibrium chemistry ::

_____ is a term used for both an electro-chemical process and a biological one. The _____ of water is the separation of water molecules into hydrogen and oxygen atoms using electricity .

21. *Answer choices:*

(see index for correct answer)

- a. Predominance diagram
- b. Multimedia fugacity model
- c. Hydrolysis
- d. Irving-Williams series

:: Polysaccharides ::

_____ is an organic compound with the formula n, a polysaccharide consisting of a linear chain of several hundred to many thousands of ß linked -glucose units. _____ is an important structural component of the primary cell wall of green plants, many forms of algae and the oomycetes. Some species of bacteria secrete it to form biofilms. _____ is the most abundant organic polymer on Earth. The _____ content of cotton fiber is 90%, that of wood is 40–50%, and that of dried hemp is approximately 57%.

Exam Probability: **High**

22. *Answer choices:*

(see index for correct answer)

- a. Mucilage
- b. Cellulose
- c. Dextrin
- d. Fucoidan

:: Reagents for organic chemistry ::

The Grignard reaction is an organometallic chemical reaction in which alkyl, vinyl, or aryl-magnesium halides add to a carbonyl group in an aldehyde or ketone. This reaction is important for the formation of carbon–carbon bonds. The reaction of an organic halide with magnesium is not a Grignard reaction, but provides a Grignard reagent.

Exam Probability: **High**

23. *Answer choices:*

(see index for correct answer)

- a. Tert-Butanesulfinamide
- b. Reagent
- c. Caesium acetate
- d. Carbonyldiimidazole

Guidance: level 1

:: Functional groups ::

_____ , also known as carbamide, is an organic compound with chemical formula CO_2. This amide has two –NH2 groups joined by a carbonyl functional group.

Exam Probability: **Medium**

24. *Answer choices:*

(see index for correct answer)

- a. Thioketal
- b. Urea
- c. Diazo
- d. Phosphaalkene

Guidance: level 1

:: Solvents ::

_____ is an organosulfur compound with the formula 2SO. This colorless liquid is an important polar aprotic solvent that dissolves both polar and nonpolar compounds and is miscible in a wide range of organic solvents as well as water. It has a relatively high melting point. DMSO has the unusual property that many individuals perceive a garlic-like taste in the mouth after contact with the skin.

Exam Probability: **Low**

25. *Answer choices:*

(see index for correct answer)

- a. 3-Mercaptopropane-1,2-diol
- b. polyethylene oxide
- c. Polyethylene glycol
- d. Dimethyl sulfoxide

:: Functional groups ::

A _____ or a hemiketal is a compound that results from the addition of an alcohol to an aldehyde or a ketone, respectively. The Greek word hèmi, meaning half, refers to the fact that a single alcohol has been added to the carbonyl group, in contrast to acetals or ketals, which are formed when a second alkoxy group has been added to the structure.

Exam Probability: **High**

26. *Answer choices:*

(see index for correct answer)

- a. Carboxamide
- b. Thiocarbamate
- c. Hemiacetal
- d. Hydrazone

:: Physical organic chemistry ::

In chemistry, the _____ is experimentally observed to have an effect of the transmission of unequal sharing of the bonding electron through a chain of atoms in a molecule, leading to a permanent dipole in a bond. It is present in a s bond as opposed to electromeric effect which is present on a p bond. All halides are electron withdrawing groups, and all alkyls are electron donating. If the electronegative atom is then joined to a chain of atoms, usually carbon, the positive charge is relayed to the other atoms in the chain. This is the electron-withdrawing _____, also known as the -I effect. In short, alkyl groups tend to donate electrons, leading to the _____.

Exam Probability: **Low**

27. *Answer choices:*

- a. Beta-silicon effect
- b. Inductive effect
- c. Polar effect
- d. Steric

Guidance: level 1

:: Inorganic phosphorus compounds ::

_____ is a colourless liquid with the formula PBr3. It is a colourless liquid that fumes in moist air due to hydrolysis and has a penetrating odour. It is used in the laboratory for the conversion of alcohols to alkyl bromides.

28. *Answer choices:*

(see index for correct answer)

- a. Phosphorus trifluoride
- b. Phosphorus triiodide
- c. Phosphorus tribromide
- d. Phosphorus pentabromide

Guidance: level 1

:: Chemistry ::

_____ , a subdiscipline of chemistry, involves the study of the relative spatial arrangement of atoms that form the structure of molecules and their manipulation. The study of _____ focuses on stereoisomers, which by definition have the same molecular formula and sequence of bonded atoms , but differ in the three-dimensional orientations of their atoms in space. For this reason, it is also known as 3D chemistry—the prefix "stereo-" means "three-dimensionality".

Exam Probability: **Low**

29. *Answer choices:*

(see index for correct answer)

- a. Green chemistry

- b. History of biochemistry
- c. Chemical similarity
- d. Free element

Guidance: level 1

:: Polymers ::

A _____ is a large molecule, or macromolecule, composed of many repeated subunits. Due to their broad range of properties, both synthetic and natural _____ s play essential and ubiquitous roles in everyday life. _____ s range from familiar synthetic plastics such as polystyrene to natural bio _____ s such as DNA and proteins that are fundamental to biological structure and function. _____ s, both natural and synthetic, are created via _____ ization of many small molecules, known as monomers. Their consequently large molecular mass relative to small molecule compounds produces unique physical properties, including toughness, viscoelasticity, and a tendency to form glasses and semicrystalline structures rather than crystals. The terms _____ and resin are often synonymous with plastic.

Exam Probability: **Low**

30. *Answer choices:*

(see index for correct answer)

- a. Ammonium polyphosphate
- b. Polyvinyl alcohol
- c. Sodium polyacrylate
- d. Polymer

:: Name reactions ::

The _____ is a chemical reaction used in organic chemistry for ring formation. It was discovered by Robert Robinson in 1935 as a method to create a six membered ring by forming three new carbon–carbon bonds. The method uses a ketone and a methyl vinyl ketone to form an a,ß-unsaturated ketone in a cyclohexane ring by a Michael addition followed by an aldol condensation. This procedure is one of the key methods to form fused ring systems.

Exam Probability: **High**

31. *Answer choices:*

(see index for correct answer)

- a. Clemmensen reduction
- b. Betti reaction
- c. Robinson annulation
- d. Bamberger triazine synthesis

:: Chelating agents ::

_____ s are cyclic chemical compounds that consist of a ring containing several ether groups. The most common _____ s are cyclic oligomers of ethylene oxide, the repeating unit being ethyleneoxy, i.e., $-CH_2CH_2O-$. Important members of this series are the tetramer , the pentamer , and the hexamer . The term "crown" refers to the resemblance between the structure of a _____ bound to a cation, and a crown sitting on a person`s head. The first number in a _____ `s name refers to the number of atoms in the cycle, and the second number refers to the number of those atoms that are oxygen. _____ s are much broader than the oligomers of ethylene oxide; an important group are derived from catechol.

Exam Probability: **Low**

32. *Answer choices:*

(see index for correct answer)

- a. 2,3-Dihydroxybenzoic acid
- b. Porphyrin
- c. Deferiprone
- d. Crown ether

Guidance: level 1

:: Cyclohexanols ::

_____ is the organic compound with the formula HOCH5. The molecule is related to cyclohexane ring by replacement of one hydrogen atom by a hydroxyl group. This compound exists as a deliquescent colorless solid with a camphor-like odor, which, when very pure, melts near room temperature. Billions of kilograms are produced annually, mainly as a precursor to nylon.

Exam Probability: **Low**

33. *Answer choices:*

(see index for correct answer)

- a. Desvenlafaxine
- b. Menthol

Guidance: level 1

:: Organobromides ::

_____ is the organobromine compound with the formula CH33Br. It is a colorless liquid, although impure samples appear yellowish. It is insoluble in water, but soluble in organic solvents. It is a primarily used as a source of the butyl group in organic synthesis. It is one of several isomers of butyl bromide.

Exam Probability: **Low**

34. *Answer choices:*

(see index for correct answer)

- a. Bromsulphthalein
- b. 1-Bromobutane
- c. Eosin B
- d. 2-Bromopropane

Guidance: level 1

:: Organic chemistry ::

_____ s are chemical reactions involving organic compounds. The basic organic chemistry reaction types are addition reactions, elimination reactions, substitution reactions, pericyclic reactions, rearrangement reactions, photochemical reactions and redox reactions. In organic synthesis, _____ s are used in the construction of new organic molecules. The production of many man-made chemicals such as drugs, plastics, food additives, fabrics depend on _____ s.

Exam Probability: **High**

35. *Answer choices:*

(see index for correct answer)

- a. Nucleofuge
- b. Aroma compound
- c. Organic reaction
- d. Pyranose

:: Physical organic chemistry ::

The _____ in organic chemistry describes a linear free-energy relationship relating reaction rates and equilibrium constants for many reactions involving benzoic acid derivatives with meta- and para-substituents to each other with just two parameters: a substituent constant and a reaction constant. This equation was developed and published by Louis Plack Hammett in 1937 as a follow-up to qualitative observations in a 1935 publication.

Exam Probability: **High**

36. *Answer choices:*

(see index for correct answer)

- a. Hammett equation
- b. Ring strain
- c. Aromatic transition state theory
- d. Nucleophile

:: Concepts in physics ::

Whether electric or magnetic, _____ s can be characterized by their _____ moment, a vector quantity. For the simple electric _____ , the electric _____ moment points from the negative charge towards the positive charge, and has a magnitude equal to the strength of each charge times the separation between the charges.

Exam Probability: **Medium**

37. *Answer choices:*

(see index for correct answer)

- a. density function
- b. Dipole
- c. kinetic theory of gases
- d. wavefunction

Guidance: level 1

:: Lipids ::

In biology and biochemistry, a _____ is a biomolecule that is soluble in nonpolar solvents. Non-polar solvents are typically hydrocarbons used to dissolve other naturally occurring hydrocarbon _____ molecules that do not dissolve in water, including fatty acids, waxes, sterols, fat-soluble vitamins , monoglycerides, diglycerides, triglycerides, and phospho _____ s.

Exam Probability: **Low**

38. *Answer choices:*

(see index for correct answer)

- a. Lipid
- b. Ceramide
- c. Salatrim
- d. Sphingosine kinase

Guidance: level 1

:: Anions ::

A _____ is an anion in which carbon is trivalent and bears a formal negative charge in at least one significant mesomeric contributor . Absent p delocalization, _____ s assume a trigonal pyramidal, bent, or linear geometry when the _____ ic carbon is bound to three , two , or one substituents, respectively. Formally, a _____ is the conjugate base of a carbon acid.

Exam Probability: **Low**

39. *Answer choices:*

(see index for correct answer)

- a. Telluride
- b. Bifluoride
- c. Carbanion
- d. Hypothiocyanite

:: Substitution reactions ::

_____ reactions are chemical reactions in which an electrophile displaces a functional group in a compound, which is typically, but not always, a hydrogen atom. Electrophilic aromatic substitution reactions are characteristic of aromatic compounds, and are important ways of introducing functional groups of benzene rings. The other main type of _____ reaction is an electrophilic aliphatic substitution reaction.

Exam Probability: **High**

40. *Answer choices:*

(see index for correct answer)

- a. Zincke reaction
- b. Oxidative decarboxylation
- c. Von Richter reaction
- d. Geminal halide hydrolysis

:: Thermochemistry ::

An _____ is a chemical reaction that releases energy through light or heat. It is the opposite of an endothermic reaction.

Exam Probability: **Low**

41. *Answer choices:*

(see index for correct answer)

- a. Standard enthalpy of formation
- b. Exothermic reaction
- c. Standard enthalpy of reaction
- d. Isodesmic reaction

Guidance: level 1

:: Protecting groups ::

In organic chemistry, _____ is the substituent or molecular fragment possessing the structure C6H5CH2–. _____ features a benzene ring attached to a CH2 group.

Exam Probability: **Low**

42. *Answer choices:*

(see index for correct answer)

- a. Carboxybenzyl
- b. Di-tert-butyl dicarbonate
- c. Tert-Butyldiphenylsilyl
- d. Acetonide

Guidance: level 1

:: Mass spectrometry ::

_____ or ionisation, is the process by which an atom or a molecule acquires a negative or positive charge by gaining or losing electrons, often in conjunction with other chemical changes. The resulting electrically charged atom or molecule is called an ion. _____ can result from the loss of an electron after collisions with subatomic particles, collisions with other atoms, molecules and ions, or through the interaction with electromagnetic radiation. Heterolytic bond cleavage and heterolytic substitution reactions can result in the formation of ion pairs. _____ can occur through radioactive decay by the internal conversion process, in which an excited nucleus transfers its energy to one of the inner-shell electrons causing it to be ejected.

Exam Probability: **Low**

43. *Answer choices:*

(see index for correct answer)

- a. Ionization
- b. Accelerator mass spectrometry
- c. Golm Metabolome Database
- d. Anode ray

:: Household chemicals ::

_____ is a simple polyol compound. It is a colorless, odorless, viscous liquid that is sweet-tasting and non-toxic. The _____ backbone is found in many lipids which are known as glycerides. It is widely used in the food industry as a sweetener and humectant in pharmaceutical formulations. _____ has three hydroxyl groups that are responsible for its solubility in water and its hygroscopic nature.

Exam Probability: **Medium**

44. *Answer choices:*

(see index for correct answer)

- a. Sodium lauroyl sarcosinate
- b. Glycerol
- c. Dioxalin
- d. Propylene glycol

:: Cations ::

A _____ is an ion with a positively charged carbon atom. Among the simplest examples are the methenium CH_3^+, methanium CH_5^+ and vinyl $C_2H_3^+$ cations. Occasionally, _____ s that bear more than one positively charged carbon atom are also encountered .

Exam Probability: Low

45. *Answer choices:*

- a. Carbocation
- b. Formamidinium
- c. Diazenylium
- d. Tetrafluoroammonium

Guidance: level 1

:: Dyes ::

_____ is an organic compound with the formula $C_6H_5NH_2$. Consisting of a phenyl group attached to an amino group, _____ is the prototypical aromatic amine. Its main use is in the manufacture of precursors to polyurethane and other industrial chemicals. Like most volatile amines, it has the odor of rotten fish. It ignites readily, burning with a smoky flame characteristic of aromatic compounds.

Exam Probability: Medium

46. *Answer choices:*

(see index for correct answer)

- a. Naphthol yellow S
- b. Aniline
- c. Squaraine dye
- d. Reactive dye

Guidance: level 1

:: Fatty acids ::

_____ is a fatty acid that occurs naturally in various animal and vegetable fats and oils. It is an odorless, colorless oil, although commercial samples may be yellowish. In chemical terms, _____ is classified as a monounsaturated omega-9 fatty acid, abbreviated with a lipid number of 18:1 cis-9. It has the formula $CH37CH=CH7COOH$. The name derives from the Latin word oleum, which means oil. It is the most common fatty acid in nature. Salts of _____ are called oleates.

Exam Probability: **Low**

47. *Answer choices:*

(see index for correct answer)

- a. Oleic acid
- b. 5-Hydroxyeicosatetraenoic acid
- c. Rumenic acid

- d. Docosatetraenoic acid

Guidance: level 1

:: Chemical reactions ::

An _____ , in organic chemistry, is in its simplest terms an organic reaction where two or more molecules combine to form a larger one .

Exam Probability: **Low**

48. *Answer choices:*

(see index for correct answer)

- a. Collision theory
- b. Addition reaction
- c. Chemical process of decomposition
- d. Acid hydrolysis

Guidance: level 1

:: Dicarboxylic acids ::

_____ is a dicarboxylic acid with the chemical formula 22. The name derives from Latin succinum, meaning amber. In living organisms, _____ takes the form of an anion, succinate, which has multiple biological roles as a metabolic intermediate being converted into fumarate by the enzyme succinate dehydrogenase in complex 2 of the electron transport chain which is involved in making ATP, and as a signaling molecule reflecting the cellular metabolic state. It is marketed as food additive E363. Succinate is generated in mitochondria via the tricarboxylic acid cycle , an energy-yielding process shared by all organisms. Succinate can exit the mitochondrial matrix and function in the cytoplasm as well as the extracellular space, changing gene expression patterns, modulating epigenetic landscape or demonstrating hormone-like signaling. As such, succinate links cellular metabolism, especially ATP formation, to the regulation of cellular function. Dysregulation of succinate synthesis, and therefore ATP synthesis, happens in some genetic mitochondrial diseases, such as Leigh syndrome, and Melas syndrome, and degradation can lead to pathological conditions, such as malignant transformation, inflammation and tissue injury.

Exam Probability: **Low**

49. *Answer choices:*

(see index for correct answer)

- a. Succinic acid
- b. Dipicolinic acid
- c. Suberic acid
- d. Chelidonic acid

Guidance: level 1

:: Pyrroles ::

_____ is a heterocyclic aromatic organic compound, a five-membered ring with the formula C4H4NH. It is a colorless volatile liquid that darkens readily upon exposure to air. Substituted derivatives are also called _____ s, e.g., N-methyl _____ , C4H4NCH3. Porphobilinogen, a trisubstituted _____ , is the biosynthetic precursor to many natural products such as heme.

Exam Probability: **High**

50. *Answer choices:*

(see index for correct answer)

- a. Coproporphyrinogens
- b. Prodigiosin
- c. Nargenicin
- d. Pyrvinium

Guidance: level 1

:: Monomers ::

_____ is an organochloride with the formula H2C=CHCl that is also called _____ monomer or chloroethene. This colorless compound is an important industrial chemical chiefly used to produce the polymer poly _____ . About 13 billion kilograms are produced annually. VCM is among the top twenty largest petrochemicals in world production. The United States currently remains the largest VCM manufacturing region because of its low-production-cost position in chlorine and ethylene raw materials. China is also a large manufacturer and one of the largest consumers of VCM. _____ is a gas with a sweet odor. It is highly toxic, flammable, and carcinogenic. It can be formed in the environment when soil organisms break down chlorinated solvents. _____ that is released by industries or formed by the breakdown of other chlorinated chemicals can enter the air and drinking water supplies. _____ is a common contaminant found near landfills. In the past VCM has been used as a refrigerant.

Exam Probability: **High**

51. *Answer choices:*

(see index for correct answer)

- a. Vinyl chloride
- b. 4-Methyl-1-pentene
- c. propylene
- d. 2,2,4,4-Tetramethyl-1,3-cyclobutanediol

Guidance: level 1

:: Carbohydrate chemistry ::

The _____ , devised by Emil Fischer in 1891, is a two-dimensional representation of a three-dimensional organic molecule by projection. _____ s were originally proposed for the depiction of carbohydrates and used by chemists, particularly in organic chemistry and biochemistry. The use of _____ s in non-carbohydrates is discouraged, as such drawings are ambiguous when confused with other types of drawing.

52. *Answer choices:*

(see index for correct answer)

- a. Disaccharide
- b. Carbohydrate conformation
- c. Glycolipid
- d. Fischer projection

Guidance: level 1

:: Reducing agents ::

_____ , also known as sodium tetrahydridoborate and sodium tetrahydroborate, is an inorganic compound with the formula $NaBH_4$. This white solid, usually encountered as a powder, is a reducing agent that finds application in chemistry, both in the laboratory and on a technical scale. It has been tested as pretreatment for pulping of wood, but is too costly to be commercialized. The compound is soluble in alcohols, certain ethers, and even water, although it slowly hydrolyzes.

53. *Answer choices:*

(see index for correct answer)

- a. Sodium borohydride
- b. Sodium cyanoborohydride
- c. SiGNa chemistry
- d. 2-Mercaptoethanol

Guidance: level 1

:: Functional groups ::

An _____ is a chemical compound derived from an oxoacid by replacing a hydroxyl group with a halide group.

Exam Probability: **Medium**

54. *Answer choices:*

(see index for correct answer)

- a. Alkyl cycloalkane
- b. Sulfenyl chloride
- c. Acylsilane
- d. Phosphate

:: Glucogenic amino acids ::

_____ is an a-amino acid that is used in the biosynthesis of proteins. It contains an amine group and a carboxylic acid group, both attached to the central carbon atom which also carries a methyl group side chain. Consequently, its IUPAC systematic name is 2-aminopropanic acid, and it is classified as a nonpolar, aliphatic a-amino acid. Under biological conditions, it exists in its zwitterionic form with its amine group protonated and its carboxyl group deprotonated . It is non-essential to humans as it can be synthesised metabolically and does not need to be present in the diet. It is encoded by all codons starting with GC .

Exam Probability: **Medium**

55. *Answer choices:*

(see index for correct answer)

- a. Threonine
- b. Cysteine
- c. Tryptophan
- d. Alanine

:: Corrosion ::

_____ is an inorganic anion of sulfur with the chemical formula S2- or a compound containing one or more S2- ions. Solutions of _____ salts are corrosive. _____ also refers to chemical compounds large families of inorganic and organic compounds, e.g. lead _____ and dimethyl _____ . Hydrogen _____ and bi _____ are the conjugate acids of _____ .

Exam Probability: **Low**

56. *Answer choices:*

(see index for correct answer)

- a. Selective leaching
- b. Bronze disease
- c. Spall
- d. Sulfide

Guidance: level 1

:: Name reactions ::

_____ is a chemical reaction described as a reduction of ketones to alkanes using zinc amalgam and concentrated hydrochloric acid. This reaction is named after Erik Christian Clemmensen, a Danish chemist.

Exam Probability: **Low**

57. *Answer choices:*

(see index for correct answer)

- a. Bechamp reduction
- b. Stickland fermentation
- c. Ruzicka large-ring synthesis
- d. Nef reaction

Guidance: level 1

:: Organohalides ::

The _____ s are a group of chemical compounds derived from alkanes containing one or more halogens. They are a subset of the general class of halocarbons, although the distinction is not often made. _____ s are widely used commercially and, consequently, are known under many chemical and commercial names. They are used as flame retardants, fire extinguishants, refrigerants, propellants, solvents, and pharmaceuticals. Subsequent to the widespread use in commerce, many halocarbons have also been shown to be serious pollutants and toxins. For example, the chlorofluorocarbons have been shown to lead to ozone depletion. Methyl bromide is a controversial fumigant. Only _____ s which contain chlorine, bromine, and iodine are a threat to the ozone layer, but fluorinated volatile _____ s in theory may have activity as greenhouse gases. Methyl iodide, a naturally occurring substance, however, does not have ozone-depleting properties and the United States Environmental Protection Agency has designated the compound a non-ozone layer depleter. For more information, see Halomethane. _____ or alkyl halides are the compounds which have the general formula "RX" where R is an alkyl or substituted alkyl group and X is a halogen .

Exam Probability: **Medium**

58. *Answer choices:*

(see index for correct answer)

- a. Acifluorfen
- b. WAY-213,613
- c. Aryl halide
- d. Haloalkane

Guidance: level 1

:: Functional groups ::

An _____ , also known as an acid _____ , is a compound with the functional group RnExNR'2 . Most common are carbox _____ s , but many other important types of _____ s are known, including phosphor _____ s and sulfon _____ s . The term _____ refers both to classes of compounds and to the functional group within those compounds.

Exam Probability: **High**

59. *Answer choices:*

(see index for correct answer)

- a. Thioketone
- b. Thioketal
- c. Amide
- d. Epoxide

Guidance: level 1

Physical chemistry

Physical chemistry is the study of macroscopic, atomic, subatomic, and particulate phenomena in chemical systems in terms of the principles, practices, and concepts of physics such as motion, energy, force, time, thermodynamics, quantum chemistry, statistical mechanics, analytical dynamics and chemical equilibrium.

:: Atoms ::

The _____ or proton number of a chemical element is the number of protons found in the nucleus of an atom. It is identical to the charge number of the nucleus. The _____ uniquely identifies a chemical element. In an uncharged atom, the _____ is also equal to the number of electrons.

Exam Probability: **Low**

1. *Answer choices:*

(see index for correct answer)

- a. Vector model of the atom
- b. Atomic number
- c. Rydberg atom
- d. Hydrogen atom

Guidance: level 1

:: Radioactivity ::

The _____ is a non-SI unit of radioactivity originally defined in 1910. According to a notice in Nature at the time, it was named in honour of Pierre _____ , but was considered at least by some to be in honour of Marie _____ as well.

Exam Probability: **Low**

2. *Answer choices:*

(see index for correct answer)

- a. Kerma
- b. Radiogenic nuclide
- c. Ionizing radiation
- d. Curie

Guidance: level 1

:: Optical filters ::

In chemistry, _____ or decadic _____ is the common logarithm of the ratio of incident to transmitted radiant power through a material, and spectral _____ or spectral decadic _____ is the common logarithm of the ratio of incident to transmitted spectral radiant power through a material. _____ is dimensionless, and in particular is not a length, though it is a monotonically increasing function of path length, and approaches zero as the path length approaches zero. The use of the term "optical density" for _____ is discouraged.In physics, a closely related quantity called "optical depth" is used instead of _____ : the natural logarithm of the ratio of incident to transmitted radiant power through a material. The optical depth equals the _____ times ln.

Exam Probability: **High**

3. *Answer choices:*

(see index for correct answer)

- a. Astronomical filter

- b. Cokin
- c. Absorbance
- d. Wratten number

Guidance: level 1

:: Subatomic particles ::

In particle physics, a _____ is a particle that follows Fermi–Dirac statistics. These particles obey the Pauli exclusion principle. _____ s include all quarks and leptons, as well as all composite particles made of an odd number of these, such as all baryons and many atoms and nuclei. _____ s differ from bosons, which obey Bose–Einstein statistics.

Exam Probability: **Low**

4. *Answer choices:*
(see index for correct answer)

- a. Relic particles
- b. Magnetic photon
- c. Fermion
- d. Photino

Guidance: level 1

:: Chemical kinetics ::

The _____ of a chemical reaction is a particular configuration along the reaction coordinate. It is defined as the state corresponding to the highest potential energy along this reaction coordinate. At this point, assuming a perfectly irreversible reaction, colliding reactant molecules always go on to form products. It is often marked with the double dagger $\ddagger$ symbol.

Exam Probability: **High**

5. *Answer choices:*

(see index for correct answer)

- a. Kinetic isotope effect
- b. Activated complex
- c. Detailed balance
- d. Transition state

Guidance: level 1

:: Chemical elements ::

_____ is a chemical element with symbol Ca and atomic number 20. As an alkaline earth metal, _____ is a reactive metal that forms a dark oxide-nitride layer when exposed to air. Its physical and chemical properties are most similar to its heavier homologues strontium and barium. It is the fifth most abundant element in Earth's crust and the third most abundant metal, after iron and aluminium. The most common _____ compound on Earth is _____ carbonate, found in limestone and the fossilised remnants of early sea life; gypsum, anhydrite, fluorite, and apatite are also sources of _____ . The name derives from Latin calx "lime", which was obtained from heating limestone.

Exam Probability: **Low**

6. *Answer choices:*

(see index for correct answer)

- a. Calcium
- b. Dysprosium
- c. Iodine
- d. Helium

Guidance: level 1

:: Crystallography ::

In physics, the _____ is the problem of loss of information concerning the phase that can occur when making a physical measurement. The name comes from the field of X-ray crystallography, where the _____ has to be solved for the determination of a structure from diffraction data. The _____ is also met in the fields of imaging and signal processing. Various approaches have been developed over the years that attempt to solve it.

Exam Probability: **Medium**

7. *Answer choices:*
(see index for correct answer)

- a. Crystallization adjutant
- b. Reciprocal lattice
- c. Mirror furnace
- d. Phase problem

Guidance: level 1

:: Scattering ::

In mechanical systems, _____ is a phenomenon that only occurs when the frequency at which a force is periodically applied is equal or nearly equal to one of the natural frequencies of the system on which it acts. This causes the system to oscillate with larger amplitude than when the force is applied at other frequencies.

Exam Probability: **Medium**

8. *Answer choices:*

(see index for correct answer)

- a. Resonance
- b. Dalitz plot
- c. High frequency approximation
- d. Low-angle laser light scattering

Guidance: level 1

:: Atomic physics ::

In atomic physics, the _____ is a physical constant and the natural unit for expressing the magnetic moment of an electron caused by either its orbital or spin angular momentum.

Exam Probability: **Medium**

9. *Answer choices:*

(see index for correct answer)

- a. Slater integrals
- b. Highly charged ion
- c. Giant resonance
- d. Bohr magneton

Guidance: level 1

:: Catalysis ::

_____ is the study of the chemical reactions that are catalysed by enzymes. In _____ , the reaction rate is measured and the effects of varying the conditions of the reaction are investigated. Studying an enzyme`s kinetics in this way can reveal the catalytic mechanism of this enzyme, its role in metabolism, how its activity is controlled, and how a drug or an agonist might inhibit the enzyme.

Exam Probability: **Low**

10. *Answer choices:*

(see index for correct answer)

- a. Catalytically perfect enzyme
- b. Catalyst support
- c. Enzyme kinetics
- d. Catalyst poisoning

Guidance: level 1

:: Amount of substance ::

The _____ is also known as the molar, universal, or ideal _____, denoted by the symbol R or R and is equivalent to the Boltzmann constant, but expressed in units of energy per temperature increment per mole, i.e. the pressure–volume product, rather than energy per temperature increment per particle. The constant is also a combination of the constants from Boyle's law, Charles's law, Avogadro's law, and Gay-Lussac's law. It is a physical constant that is featured in many fundamental equations in the physical sciences, such as the ideal gas law and the Nernst equation.

Exam Probability: **High**

11. *Answer choices:*

(see index for correct answer)

- a. Colligative
- b. Avogadro's law

Guidance: level 1

:: Desiccants ::

_____ is a chemical element with symbol K and atomic number 19. _____ is a silvery-white metal that is soft enough to be cut with a knife, with little force. _____ metal reacts rapidly with atmospheric oxygen to form flaky white _____ peroxide in only seconds of exposure. It was first isolated from potash, the ashes of plants, from which its name derives. In the periodic table, _____ is one of the alkali metals, all of which have a single valence electron in the outer electron shell, that is easily removed to create an ion with a positive charge – a cation, that combines with anions to form salts. _____ in nature occurs only in ionic salts. Elemental _____ reacts vigorously with water, generating sufficient heat to ignite hydrogen emitted in the reaction, and burning with a lilac-colored flame. It is found dissolved in sea water , and occurs in many minerals such as orthoclase, a common constituent of granites and other igneous rocks.

Exam Probability: **Low**

12. *Answer choices:*

(see index for correct answer)

- a. Silica gel
- b. Desiccant
- c. Potassium carbonate
- d. Drierite

Guidance: level 1

:: Chemical engineering ::

_____ or equilibrium _____ is defined as the pressure exerted by a vapor in thermodynamic equilibrium with its condensed phases at a given temperature in a closed system. The equilibrium _____ is an indication of a liquid's evaporation rate. It relates to the tendency of particles to escape from the liquid . A substance with a high _____ at normal temperatures is often referred to as volatile. The pressure exhibited by vapor present above a liquid surface is known as _____ . As the temperature of a liquid increases, the kinetic energy of its molecules also increases. As the kinetic energy of the molecules increases, the number of molecules transitioning into a vapor also increases, thereby increasing the _____ .

Exam Probability: **Medium**

13. *Answer choices:*

(see index for correct answer)

- a. Accidental release source terms
- b. Fluid dynamics
- c. Vapor pressure
- d. Industrial gas

Guidance: level 1

:: Photochemistry ::

_____ is a pump-probe laboratory technique, in which a sample is firstly excited by a strong pulse of light from a laser of nanosecond, picosecond, or femtosecond pulse width or by a short-pulse light source such as a flash lamp. This first strong pulse starts a chemical reaction or leads to an increased population for energy levels other than the ground state within a sample of atoms or molecules. Typically the absorption of light by the sample is recorded within short time intervals to monitor relaxation or reaction processes initiated by the pump pulse.

Exam Probability: **Low**

14. *Answer choices:*

(see index for correct answer)

- a. Photochemical reactions
- b. Flash photolysis
- c. Joint Center for Artificial Photosynthesis
- d. Direct DNA damage

Guidance: level 1

:: Quantum chemistry ::

_____ s are functions used as atomic orbitals in the linear combination of atomic orbitals molecular orbital method. They are named after the physicist John C. Slater, who introduced them in 1930.

Exam Probability: **Medium**

15. *Answer choices:*

(see index for correct answer)

- a. STO-nG basis sets
- b. CHELPG
- c. Slater-type orbital
- d. Basis set superposition error

Guidance: level 1

:: Electrodes ::

A _____ is a type of ion-selective electrode made of a doped glass membrane that is sensitive to a specific ion. The most common application of ion-selective _____ s is for the measurement of pH. The pH electrode is an example of a _____ that is sensitive to hydrogen ions. _____ s play an important part in the instrumentation for chemical analysis and physico-chemical studies. The voltage of the _____ , relative to some reference value, is sensitive to changes in the activity of certain type of ions.

Exam Probability: **Medium**

16. *Answer choices:*

(see index for correct answer)

- a. Palladium-hydrogen electrode
- b. Chemically modified electrode

- c. Clark electrode
- d. Saturated calomel electrode

Guidance: level 1

:: Gases ::

In physics, a _____ is a theoretical gas model that differs from real gases in ways that makes certain calculations easier to handle. Its behaviour is also simplified compared to an ideal gas . In _____ models, intermolecular forces are neglected. This means that one can neglect many complications that may arise from the Van der Waals forces.

Exam Probability: **Low**

17. *Answer choices:*
(see index for correct answer)

- a. Silane
- b. Gas exchange
- c. Gas leak
- d. Perfect gas

Guidance: level 1

:: Cubic minerals ::

_____ is a chemical element with symbol Fe and atomic number 26. It is a metal, that belongs to the first transition series and group 8 of the periodic table. It is by mass the most common element on Earth, forming much of Earth's outer and inner core. It is the fourth most common element in the Earth's crust.

Exam Probability: **Medium**

18. *Answer choices:*

(see index for correct answer)

- a. Domeykite
- b. Fluorite
- c. Iron
- d. Hauyne

Guidance: level 1

:: Chemical elements ::

_____ is a chemical element with symbol N and atomic number 7. It was first discovered and isolated by Scottish physician Daniel Rutherford in 1772. Although Carl Wilhelm Scheele and Henry Cavendish had independently done so at about the same time, Rutherford is generally accorded the credit because his work was published first. The name nitrogène was suggested by French chemist Jean-Antoine-Claude Chaptal in 1790, when it was found that _____ was present in nitric acid and nitrates. Antoine Lavoisier suggested instead the name azote, from the Greek t "no life", as it is an asphyxiant gas; this name is instead used in many languages, such as French, Russian, Romanian and Turkish, and appears in the English names of some _____ compounds such as hydrazine, azides and azo compounds.

Exam Probability: **Medium**

19. *Answer choices:*

(see index for correct answer)

- a. Nitrogen
- b. Ununpentium
- c. Unbinilium
- d. Thorium

Guidance: level 1

:: Gases ::

_____ es are non-hypothetical gases whose molecules occupy space and have interactions; consequently, they adhere to gas laws. To understand the behaviour of _____ es, the following must be taken into account.

20. *Answer choices:*

(see index for correct answer)

- a. Carbon monoxide poisoning
- b. Selenoyl fluoride
- c. Real gas
- d. Monatomic gas

Guidance: level 1

:: Phase transitions ::

_____ , or fusion, is a physical process that results in the phase transition of a substance from a solid to a liquid. This occurs when the internal energy of the solid increases, typically by the application of heat or pressure, which increases the substance's temperature to the _____ point. At the _____ point, the ordering of ions or molecules in the solid breaks down to a less ordered state, and the solid melts to become a liquid.

Exam Probability: **Medium**

21. *Answer choices:*

(see index for correct answer)

- a. Bubble point
- b. Phase boundary

- c. Abelian sandpile model
- d. Literature of phase boundaries

Guidance: level 1

:: Quantum mechanics ::

The _____ of a quantum-mechanical system is its lowest-energy state; the energy of the _____ is known as the zero-point energy of the system. An is any state with energy greater than the _____ . In the quantum field theory, the _____ is usually called the vacuum state or the vacuum.

Exam Probability: **Medium**

22. *Answer choices:*

(see index for correct answer)

- a. Many-body problem
- b. Excited state
- c. Ground state
- d. Calogero conjecture

Guidance: level 1

:: Atomic physics ::

In quantum mechanics, the _____ is one of four quantum numbers which are assigned to all electrons in an atom to describe that electron's state. As a discrete variable, the _____ is always an integer. As n increases, the number of electronic shells increases and the electron spends more time farther from the nucleus. As n increases, the electron is also at a higher energy and is, therefore, less tightly bound to the nucleus. The total energy of an electron, as described below, is a negative inverse quadratic function of the _____ n.

Exam Probability: **Low**

23. *Answer choices:*

(see index for correct answer)

- a. Quadrupole splitting
- b. Atomic fountain
- c. Magnetic trap
- d. Autoionization

Guidance: level 1

:: Superconductivity ::

The _____ is the expulsion of a magnetic field from a superconductor during its transition to the superconducting state. The German physicists Walther Meissner and Robert Ochsenfeld discovered this phenomenon in 1933 by measuring the magnetic field distribution outside superconducting tin and lead samples. The samples, in the presence of an applied magnetic field, were cooled below their superconducting transition temperature, whereupon the samples cancelled nearly all interior magnetic fields. They detected this effect only indirectly because the magnetic flux is conserved by a superconductor: when the interior field decreases, the exterior field increases. The experiment demonstrated for the first time that superconductors were more than just perfect conductors and provided a uniquely defining property of the superconductor state. The ability for the expulsion effect is determined by the nature of equilibrium formed by the neutralization within the unit cell of a superconductor.

Exam Probability: **High**

24. *Answer choices:*

(see index for correct answer)

- a. Meissner effect
- b. Flux pinning
- c. Residual-resistance ratio
- d. Type-II superconductor

Guidance: level 1

:: Chemical reactions ::

In chemical kinetics, the overall rate of a reaction is often approximately determined by the slowest step, known as the _________ or rate-limiting step. For a given reaction mechanism, the prediction of the corresponding rate equation is often simplified by using this approximation of the _________.

Exam Probability: **Low**

25. *Answer choices:*

(see index for correct answer)

- a. Self-assembling peptide
- b. Bioorthogonal chemistry
- c. Chloro-5-substituted adamantyl-1,2-dioxetane phosphate
- d. Rate-determining step

Guidance: level 1

:: Chemical elements ::

_____ is a chemical element with symbol He and atomic number 2. It is a colorless, odorless, tasteless, non-toxic, inert, monatomic gas, the first in the noble gas group in the periodic table. Its boiling point is the lowest among all the elements. After hydrogen, _____ is the second lightest and second most abundant element in the observable universe, being present at about 24% of the total elemental mass, which is more than 12 times the mass of all the heavier elements combined. Its abundance is similar to this figure in the Sun and in Jupiter. This is due to the very high nuclear binding energy of _____ -4 with respect to the next three elements after _____ . This _____ -4 binding energy also accounts for why it is a product of both nuclear fusion and radioactive decay. Most _____ in the universe is _____ -4, the vast majority of which was formed during the Big Bang. Large amounts of new _____ are being created by nuclear fusion of hydrogen in stars.

Exam Probability: **Low**

26. *Answer choices:*

(see index for correct answer)

- a. Hassium
- b. Helium
- c. Cerium
- d. Europium

Guidance: level 1

:: Gas laws ::

The _____ were developed at the end of the 18th century, when scientists began to realize that relationships between pressure, volume and temperature of a sample of gas could be obtained which would hold to approximation for all gases. Gases behave in a similar way over a wide variety of conditions because they all have molecules which are widely spaced, and the equation of state for an ideal gas is derived from kinetic theory. The earlier _____ are now considered as special cases of the ideal gas equation, with one or more variables held constant.

Exam Probability: **Low**

27. *Answer choices:*

(see index for correct answer)

- a. Van der Waals constants
- b. Combined gas law
- c. Ideal gas law
- d. Gas laws

Guidance: level 1

:: Thermodynamics ::

Though subject internally to its own gravity, an _____ is usually taken to be outside the reach of external gravitational and other long-range forces.

Exam Probability: **Medium**

28. *Answer choices:*

(see index for correct answer)

- a. Sand bath
- b. Reduced properties
- c. Thermodynamic length
- d. Isolated system

Guidance: level 1

:: Polymers ::

A _____ is a large molecule, or macromolecule, composed of many repeated subunits. Due to their broad range of properties, both synthetic and natural _____ s play essential and ubiquitous roles in everyday life. _____ s range from familiar synthetic plastics such as polystyrene to natural bio _____ s such as DNA and proteins that are fundamental to biological structure and function. _____ s, both natural and synthetic, are created via _____ ization of many small molecules, known as monomers. Their consequently large molecular mass relative to small molecule compounds produces unique physical properties, including toughness, viscoelasticity, and a tendency to form glasses and semicrystalline structures rather than crystals. The terms _____ and resin are often synonymous with plastic.

Exam Probability: **High**

29. *Answer choices:*

(see index for correct answer)

- a. Polymer engineering
- b. Santoprene
- c. Parylene
- d. Aquamelt

Guidance: level 1

:: Equilibrium chemistry ::

The _____ of a chemical reaction is the value of its reaction quotient at chemical equilibrium, a state approached by a dynamic chemical system after sufficient time has elapsed at which its composition has no measurable tendency towards further change. For a given set of reaction conditions, the _____ is independent of the initial analytical concentrations of the reactant and product species in the mixture. Thus, given the initial composition of a system, known _____ values can be used to determine the composition of the system at equilibrium. However, reaction parameters like temperature, solvent, and ionic strength may all influence the value of the _____ .

Exam Probability: **Medium**

30. *Answer choices:*

(see index for correct answer)

- a. Equilibrium constant
- b. Reversible reaction
- c. Wong-Sandler mixing rule
- d. Dissociation

:: Bases ::

_____ is a diatomic anion with chemical formula OH-. It consists of an oxygen and hydrogen atom held together by a covalent bond, and carries a negative electric charge. It is an important but usually minor constituent of water. It functions as a base, a ligand, a nucleophile, and a catalyst. The _____ ion forms salts, some of which dissociate in aqueous solution, liberating solvated _____ ions. Sodium _____ is a multi-million-ton per annum commodity chemical. A _____ attached to a strongly electropositive center may itself ionize, liberating a hydrogen cation , making the parent compound an acid.

Exam Probability: **Low**

31. *Answer choices:*

(see index for correct answer)

- a. Hydroxide
- b. Soluene
- c. Strontium hydroxide
- d. Lewis base

:: Equilibrium chemistry ::

In chemistry, a _____ is a function of the activities or concentrations of the chemical species involved in a chemical reaction. In the special case that the reaction is at equilibrium the _____ is constant and equal to the equilibrium constant that appears in the expression of the law of mass action.

Exam Probability: **Low**

32. *Answer choices:*
(see index for correct answer)

- a. Partial pressure
- b. Reaction quotient
- c. Homoassociation
- d. Thermodynamic equilibrium

Guidance: level 1

:: Atomic physics ::

_____ is the ability to form instantaneous dipoles. It is a property of matter. Polarizabilities determine the dynamical response of a bound system to external fields, and provide insight into a molecule's internal structure. In a solid, _____ is defined as dipole moment per unit volume of the crystal cell.

Exam Probability: **Low**

33. *Answer choices:*

(see index for correct answer)

- a. Hanle effect
- b. Scattering
- c. Magnetic trap
- d. Polarizability

Guidance: level 1

:: Length ::

In physics, the _____ is the spatial period of a periodic wave—the distance over which the wave's shape repeats. It is thus the inverse of the spatial frequency. _____ is usually determined by considering the distance between consecutive corresponding points of the same phase, such as crests, troughs, or zero crossings and is a characteristic of both traveling waves and standing waves, as well as other spatial wave patterns. _____ is commonly designated by the Greek letter lambda . The term _____ is also sometimes applied to modulated waves, and to the sinusoidal envelopes of modulated waves or waves formed by interference of several sinusoids.

Exam Probability: **High**

34. *Answer choices:*

(see index for correct answer)

- a. radius
- b. Wavelength

- c. radii

Guidance: level 1

:: Physical chemistry ::

_____ occurs when an electron relocates from an atom or molecule to another such chemical entity. ET is a mechanistic description of a redox reaction, wherein the oxidation state of reactant and product changes. _____ is ionic bonding.

Exam Probability: **Medium**

35. *Answer choices:*
(see index for correct answer)

- a. Electron transfer
- b. Sticking probability
- c. Atomic ratio
- d. Lamellar structure

Guidance: level 1

:: Atomic physics ::

The _____ is a physical constant, approximately equal to the most probable distance between the nucleus and the electron in a hydrogen atom in its ground state. It is named after Niels Bohr, due to its role in the Bohr model of an atom. Its value is $5.2917721067 \times 10^{-11}$ m.

Exam Probability: **Low**

36. *Answer choices:*

(see index for correct answer)

- a. Bohr radius
- b. Resolved sideband cooling
- c. Electron beam ion source
- d. Solid harmonics

Guidance: level 1

:: Chemical elements ::

_____ is a chemical element with symbol V and atomic number 23. It is a hard, silvery-grey, ductile, malleable transition metal. The elemental metal is rarely found in nature, but once isolated artificially, the formation of an oxide layer somewhat stabilizes the free metal against further oxidation.

Exam Probability: **Low**

37. *Answer choices:*

(see index for correct answer)

- a. Curium
- b. Cerium
- c. Ununennium
- d. Vanadium

Guidance: level 1

:: Spectrometers ::

A _____ is a scientific instrument used to separate and measure spectral components of a physical phenomenon. _____ is a broad term often used to describe instruments that measure a continuous variable of a phenomenon where the spectral components are somehow mixed. In visible light a _____ can for instance separate white light and measure individual narrow bands of color, called a spectrum, while a mass _____ measures the spectrum of the masses of the atoms or molecules present in a gas. The first _____ s were used to split light into an array of separate colors. _____ s were developed in early studies of physics, astronomy, and chemistry. The capability of spectroscopy to determine chemical composition drove its advancement and continues to be one of its primary uses. _____ s are used in astronomy to analyze the chemical composition of stars and planets, and _____ s gather data on the origin of the universe.

Exam Probability: **Low**

38. *Answer choices:*

(see index for correct answer)

- a. Spectrometer
- b. Bonner sphere
- c. Tropospheric Emission Spectrometer
- d. Image mapping spectrometer

Guidance: level 1

:: Equilibrium chemistry ::

_____ is an axiomatic concept of thermodynamics. It is an internal state of a single thermodynamic system, or a relation between several thermodynamic systems connected by more or less permeable or impermeable walls. In _____ there are no net macroscopic flows of matter or of energy, either within a system or between systems. In a system in its own state of internal _____ , no macroscopic change occurs. Systems in mutual _____ are simultaneously in mutual thermal, mechanical, chemical, and radiative equilibria. Systems can be in one kind of mutual equilibrium, though not in others. In _____ , all kinds of equilibrium hold at once and indefinitely, until disturbed by a thermodynamic operation. In a macroscopic equilibrium, almost or perfectly exactly balanced microscopic exchanges occur; this is the physical explanation of the notion of macroscopic equilibrium.

Exam Probability: **High**

39. *Answer choices:*

(see index for correct answer)

- a. Thermodynamic equilibrium
- b. Hand boiler

- c. Binding selectivity
- d. Isohydric principle

Guidance: level 1

:: Carbon forms ::

_____ , archaically referred to as plumbago, is a crystalline form of the element carbon with its atoms arranged in a hexagonal structure. It occurs naturally in this form and is the most stable form of carbon under standard conditions. Under high pressures and temperatures it converts to diamond. _____ is used in pencils and lubricants. Its high conductivity makes it useful in electronic products such as electrodes, batteries, and solar panels.

Exam Probability: **High**

40. *Answer choices:*

(see index for correct answer)

- a. Bilayer graphene
- b. Carbon
- c. Aggregated diamond nanorod
- d. Graphite

Guidance: level 1

:: Quantum chemistry ::

In quantum mechanics, a _____ is an expression that describes the wave function of a multi-fermionic system that satisfies anti-symmetry requirements, and consequently the Pauli principle, by changing sign upon exchange of two electrons . Only a small subset of all possible fermionic wave functions can be written as a single _____ , but those form an important and useful subset because of their simplicity.

Exam Probability: **Medium**

41. *Answer choices:*

(see index for correct answer)

- a. Hartree product
- b. Size consistency
- c. Slater determinant
- d. DIIS

Guidance: level 1

:: Materials science ::

_____ , or DSC, is a thermoanalytical technique in which the difference in the amount of heat required to increase the temperature of a sample and reference is measured as a function of temperature. Both the sample and reference are maintained at nearly the same temperature throughout the experiment. Generally, the temperature program for a DSC analysis is designed such that the sample holder temperature increases linearly as a function of time. The reference sample should have a well-defined heat capacity over the range of temperatures to be scanned.

42. *Answer choices:*

(see index for correct answer)

- a. Thermogravimetric analysis
- b. Friability
- c. Differential scanning calorimetry
- d. Tribometer

Guidance: level 1

:: Nucleic acids ::

A _____ is a unit consisting of two nucleobases bound to each other by hydrogen bonds. They form the building blocks of the DNA double helix and contribute to the folded structure of both DNA and RNA. Dictated by specific hydrogen bonding patterns, Watson–Crick _____ s allow the DNA helix to maintain a regular helical structure that is subtly dependent on its nucleotide sequence. The complementary nature of this based-paired structure provides a redundant copy of the genetic information encoded within each strand of DNA. The regular structure and data redundancy provided by the DNA double helix make DNA well suited to the storage of genetic information, while base-pairing between DNA and incoming nucleotides provides the mechanism through which DNA polymerase replicates DNA and RNA polymerase transcribes DNA into RNA. Many DNA-binding proteins can recognize specific base-pairing patterns that identify particular regulatory regions of genes.

Exam Probability: **High**

43. *Answer choices:*

(see index for correct answer)

- a. Genomic signature
- b. National Institute of Genetics
- c. Oligonucleotide
- d. Spherical nucleic acid

Guidance: level 1

:: Spectroscopy ::

In spectroscopy, _____ is a dimensionless quantity that expresses the probability of absorption or emission of electromagnetic radiation in transitions between energy levels of an atom or molecule. The _____ can be thought of as the ratio between the quantum mechanical transition rate and the classical absorption/emission rate of a single electron oscillator with the same frequency as the transition.

Exam Probability: **High**

44. *Answer choices:*

(see index for correct answer)

- a. Oscillator strength
- b. Photoluminescence
- c. Photoacoustic effect
- d. Reststrahlen effect

:: Quantum chemistry ::

The _____ , named after physicist Philip M. Morse, is a convenient interatomic interaction model for the potential energy of a diatomic molecule. It is a better approximation for the vibrational structure of the molecule than the QHO because it explicitly includes the effects of bond breaking, such as the existence of unbound states. It also accounts for the anharmonicity of real bonds and the non-zero transition probability for overtone and combination bands. The _____ can also be used to model other interactions such as the interaction between an atom and a surface. Due to its simplicity , it is not used in modern spectroscopy. However, its mathematical form inspired the MLR potential, which is the most popular potential energy function used for fitting spectroscopic data.

Exam Probability: **Low**

45. *Answer choices:*

(see index for correct answer)

- a. Conical intersection
- b. Frontier molecular orbital theory
- c. Spin transition
- d. Gaussian quantum Monte Carlo

:: Thermochemistry ::

An _____ is a chemical reaction that releases energy through light or heat. It is the opposite of an endothermic reaction.

Exam Probability: **Medium**

46. *Answer choices:*

(see index for correct answer)

- a. Exothermic reaction
- b. Latent heat
- c. Nernst heat theorem
- d. Principle of maximum work

Guidance: level 1

:: Equilibrium chemistry ::

In a mixture of gases, each constituent gas has a _____ which is the notional pressure of that constituent gas if it alone occupied the entire volume of the original mixture at the same temperature. The total pressure of an ideal gas mixture is the sum of the _____ s of the gases in the mixture.

Exam Probability: **High**

47. *Answer choices:*

(see index for correct answer)

- a. Specific ion interaction theory
- b. Binding selectivity
- c. Partial pressure
- d. Ion-association

Guidance: level 1

:: Spectroscopy ::

The _____ is the shifting and splitting of spectral lines of atoms and molecules due to the presence of an external electric field. It is the electric-field analogue of the Zeeman effect, where a spectral line is split into several components due to the presence of the magnetic field. Although initially coined for the static case, it is also used in the wider context to describe effect of time-dependent electric fields. In particular, the _____ is responsible for the pressure broadening of spectral lines by charged particles in plasmas. For majority of spectral lines, the _____ is either linear or quadratic with a high accuracy.

Exam Probability: **Medium**

48. *Answer choices:*

(see index for correct answer)

- a. Immobilized enzyme ESR
- b. Stark effect

- c. Opacity
- d. Acoustic paramagnetic resonance

Guidance: level 1

:: Condensed matter physics ::

In electromagnetism, absolute _____ , often simply called _____ , usually denoted by the Greek letter e , is the measure of capacitance that is encountered when forming an electric field in a particular medium. More specifically, _____ describes the amount of charge needed to generate one unit of electric flux in a particular medium. Accordingly, a charge will yield more electric flux in a medium with low _____ than in a medium with high _____ . _____ is the measure of a material's ability to store an electric field in the polarization of the medium.

Exam Probability: **Low**

49. *Answer choices:*
(see index for correct answer)

- a. Magnetocapacitance
- b. Permittivity
- c. Spaser
- d. Doping

Guidance: level 1

:: Atomic physics ::

The _____ is commonly used in thermodynamics, to simplify certain equations. It has units of temperature and is defined as

Exam Probability: **Low**

50. *Answer choices:*

(see index for correct answer)

- a. Boson
- b. Electric field gradient
- c. Solid harmonics
- d. Vibrational temperature

Guidance: level 1

:: Corrosion ::

_____ is an inorganic anion of sulfur with the chemical formula $S2-$ or a compound containing one or more $S2-$ ions. Solutions of _____ salts are corrosive. _____ also refers to chemical compounds large families of inorganic and organic compounds, e.g. lead _____ and dimethyl _____ . Hydrogen _____ and bi _____ are the conjugate acids of _____ .

Exam Probability: **Low**

51. *Answer choices:*

- a. Tetrathionate
- b. Sulfide
- c. Corrosion fatigue
- d. Pitting Resistance Equivalent Number

Guidance: level 1

:: Spectroscopy ::

A _____ is an optical device that transmits a mechanically selectable narrow band of wavelengths of light or other radiation chosen from a wider range of wavelengths available at the input. The name is from the Greek roots mono-, "single", and chroma, "colour", and the Latin suffix -ator, denoting an agent.

Exam Probability: **Medium**

52. *Answer choices:*

- a. Reststrahlen effect
- b. Transmittance
- c. GF method
- d. Surface selection rule

:: Chemical reactions ::

_____ , also known as reaction kinetics, is the study of rates of chemical processes. _____ includes investigations of how different experimental conditions can influence the speed of a chemical reaction and yield information about the reaction`s mechanism and transition states, as well as the construction of mathematical models that can describe the characteristics of a chemical reaction.

Exam Probability: **Medium**

53. *Answer choices:*

(see index for correct answer)

- a. Combination reaction
- b. Chemical kinetics
- c. Electrophilic addition
- d. Comproportionation

:: Spectroscopy ::

The _____ of a radiation-induced process is the number of times a specific event occurs per photon absorbed by the system. The "event" is typically a kind of chemical reaction.

Exam Probability: **Medium**

54. *Answer choices:*

(see index for correct answer)

- a. Golay cell
- b. Quantum yield
- c. Slope spectroscopy
- d. Diffusing-wave spectroscopy

Guidance: level 1

:: Inorganic amines ::

_____ is a compound of nitrogen and hydrogen with the formula NH_3. The simplest pnictogen hydride, _____ is a colourless gas with a characteristic pungent smell. It is a common nitrogenous waste, particularly among aquatic organisms, and it contributes significantly to the nutritional needs of terrestrial organisms by serving as a precursor to food and fertilizers. _____ , either directly or indirectly, is also a building block for the synthesis of many pharmaceutical products and is used in many commercial cleaning products. It is mainly collected by downward displacement of both air and water. _____ is named for the _____ ns, worshipers of the Egyptian god Amun, who used ammonium chloride in their rituals.

55. *Answer choices:*

(see index for correct answer)

- a. Nitrogen trifluoride
- b. Nitrogen triiodide
- c. Nitrogen tribromide
- d. Hydroxylamine

Guidance: level 1

:: Emission spectroscopy ::

In physics and chemistry, the _____ is a hydrogen spectral series of transitions and resulting ultraviolet emission lines of the hydrogen atom as an electron goes from $n = 2$ to $n = 1$, the lowest energy level of the electron. The transitions are named sequentially by Greek letters: from $n = 2$ to $n = 1$ is called Lyman-alpha, 3 to 1 is Lyman-beta, 4 to 1 is Lyman-gamma, and so on. The series is named after its discoverer, Theodore Lyman. The greater the difference in the principal quantum numbers, the higher the energy of the electromagnetic emission.

Exam Probability: **Medium**

56. *Answer choices:*

(see index for correct answer)

- a. Isotopic shift
- b. Inverse photoemission spectroscopy
- c. Gaussian broadening
- d. Lyman series

Guidance: level 1

:: Light ::

The _____ in vacuum, commonly denoted c, is a universal physical constant important in many areas of physics. Its exact value is 299,792,458 metres per second . It is exact because by international agreement a metre is defined as the length of the path travelled by light in vacuum during a time interval of 1/299792458 second. According to special relativity, c is the maximum speed at which all conventional matter and hence all known forms of information in the universe can travel. Though this speed is most commonly associated with light, it is in fact the speed at which all massless particles and changes of the associated fields travel in vacuum . Such particles and waves travel at c regardless of the motion of the source or the inertial reference frame of the observer. In the special and general theories of relativity, c interrelates space and time, and also appears in the famous equation of mass–energy equivalence $E = mc2$.

Exam Probability: **High**

57. *Answer choices:*

(see index for correct answer)

- a. Moonlight
- b. Angular momentum of light

- c. SMARTS
- d. Speed of light

Guidance: level 1

:: Acid-base chemistry ::

An _____ is a molecule or ion capable of donating a hydron , or, alternatively, capable of forming a covalent bond with an electron pair .

Exam Probability: **Low**

58. *Answer choices:*

(see index for correct answer)

- a. Acid
- b. Monobasic acid
- c. Charlot equation
- d. Conjugate acid

Guidance: level 1

:: Chemical kinetics ::

_____ is defined in chemical kinetics and collision theory, in the background of theoretical kinetics.

Exam Probability: **High**

59. *Answer choices:*

(see index for correct answer)

- a. Kinetic isotope effect
- b. Pressure jump
- c. Surface-area-to-volume ratio
- d. Collision frequency

Guidance: level 1

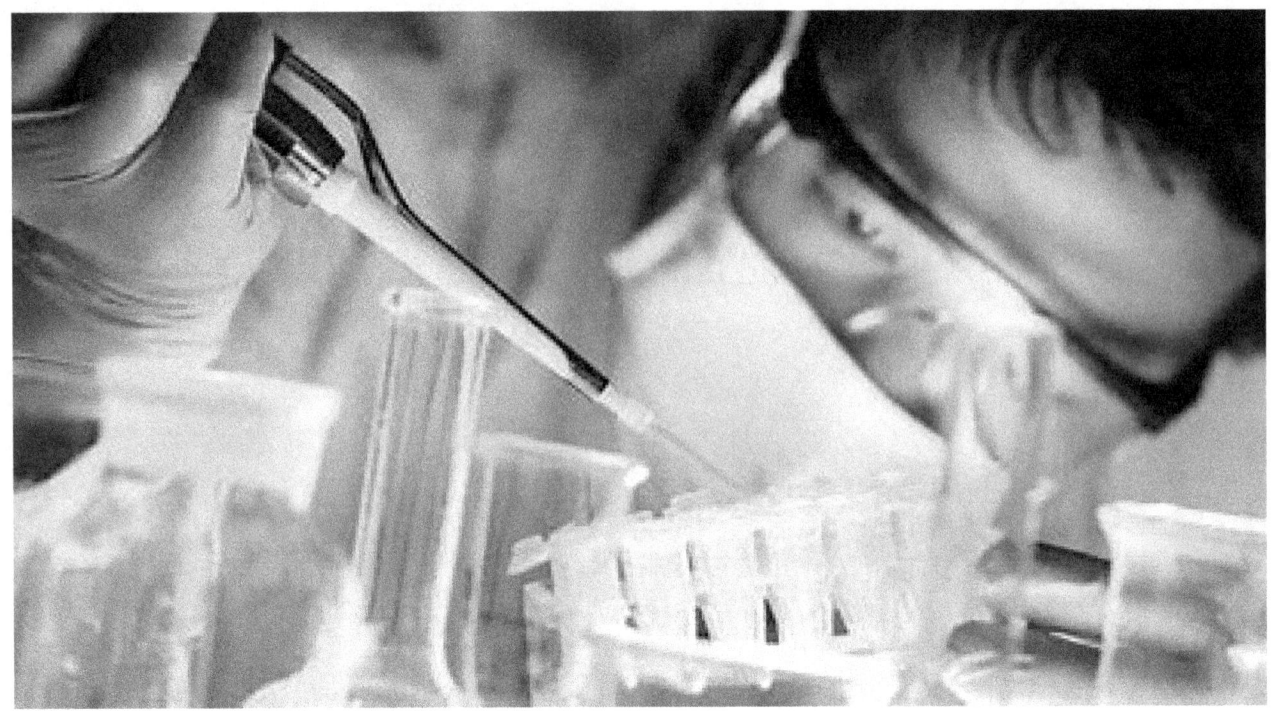

Chemical engineering

Chemical engineering is a branch of engineering that uses principles of chemistry, physics, mathematics, and economics to efficiently use, produce, transform, and transport chemicals, materials, and energy. A chemical engineer designs large-scale processes that convert chemicals, raw materials, living cells, microorganisms, and energy into useful forms and products.

:: Thermodynamics ::

_____ or thermal flux, sometimes also referred to as _____ density or heat flow rate intensity is a flow of energy per unit of area per unit of time. In SI its units are watts per square metre . It has both a direction and a magnitude, and so it is a vector quantity. To define the _____ at a certain point in space, one takes the limiting case where the size of the surface becomes infinitesimally small.

Exam Probability: **Medium**

1. *Answer choices:*

(see index for correct answer)

- a. Scale of temperature
- b. Exergonic
- c. Scuderi cycle
- d. Heat flux

Guidance: level 1

:: Industrial ecology ::

_____ is a strategy for reducing the amount of waste created and released into the environment, particularly by industrial facilities, agriculture, or consumers. Many large corporations view P2 as a method of improving the efficiency and profitability of production processes by technology advancements. Legislative bodies have enacted P2 measures, such as the _____ Act of 1990 and the Clean Air Act Amendments of 1990 by the United States Congress.

2. *Answer choices:*

(see index for correct answer)

- a. Pollution prevention
- b. Zero waste
- c. Source reduction
- d. Eco-costs

Guidance: level 1

:: Separation processes ::

_____ is the tendency for particles in suspension to settle out of the fluid in which they are entrained and come to rest against a barrier. This is due to their motion through the fluid in response to the forces acting on them: these forces can be due to gravity, centrifugal acceleration, or electromagnetism. In geology, _____ is often used as the opposite of erosion, i.e., the terminal end of sediment transport. In that sense, it includes the termination of transport by saltation or true bedload transport. Settling is the falling of suspended particles through the liquid, whereas _____ is the termination of the settling process. In estuarine environments, settling can be influenced by the presence or absence of vegetation. Trees such as mangroves are crucial to the attenuation of waves or currents, promoting the settlement of suspended particles.

Exam Probability: **High**

3. *Answer choices:*

(see index for correct answer)

- a. Protein skimmer
- b. Counterflow centrifugation elutriation
- c. Sedimentation
- d. Dewatering screw press

Guidance: level 1

:: Chemical processes ::

_____ is the process by which air is circulated through, mixed with or dissolved in a liquid or substance.

Exam Probability: **High**

4. *Answer choices:*

(see index for correct answer)

- a. Aeration
- b. Aludel
- c. Kraft process
- d. Cryogenic oxygen plant

Guidance: level 1

:: Phase transitions ::

_____ is the change of the physical state of matter from the gas phase into the liquid phase, and is the reverse of vaporisation. The word most often refers to the water cycle. It can also be defined as the change in the state of water vapour to liquid water when in contact with a liquid or solid surface or cloud _____ nuclei within the atmosphere. When the transition happens from the gaseous phase into the solid phase directly, the change is called deposition.

Exam Probability: **High**

5. *Answer choices:*

(see index for correct answer)

- a. Condensation
- b. Diffusionless transformation
- c. Curie temperature
- d. Spinodal decomposition

Guidance: level 1

:: Drying ::

_____ is a mass transfer process consisting of the removal of water or another solvent by evaporation from a solid, semi-solid or liquid. This process is often used as a final production step before selling or packaging products. To be considered "dried", the final product must be solid, in the form of a continuous sheet , long pieces , particles or powder . A source of heat and an agent to remove the vapor produced by the process are often involved. In bioproducts like food, grains, and pharmaceuticals like vaccines, the solvent to be removed is almost invariably water. Desiccation may be synonymous with _____ or considered an extreme form of _____ .

Exam Probability: **Medium**

6. *Answer choices:*

(see index for correct answer)

- a. Drying
- b. Whalenburg Stack Dryer

Guidance: level 1

:: Thin films ::

A _____ is a layer of material ranging from fractions of a nanometer to several micrometers in thickness. The controlled synthesis of materials as _____ s is a fundamental step in many applications. A familiar example is the household mirror, which typically has a thin metal coating on the back of a sheet of glass to form a reflective interface. The process of silvering was once commonly used to produce mirrors, while more recently the metal layer is deposited using techniques such as sputtering. Advances in _____ deposition techniques during the 20th century have enabled a wide range of technological breakthroughs in areas such as magnetic recording media, electronic semiconductor devices, LEDs, optical coatings , hard coatings on cutting tools, and for both energy generation and storage . It is also being applied topharmaceuticals, via thin-film drug delivery. A stack of _____ s is called a multilayer.

Exam Probability: **High**

7. *Answer choices:*

(see index for correct answer)

- a. Perfluorodecyltrichlorosilane
- b. Thin film
- c. Plasma-immersion ion implantation
- d. Octadecyltrichlorosilane

Guidance: level 1

:: Polymer chemistry ::

The _____ is a dimensionless number related to heat conduction from a wall to a flowing viscous fluid, commonly used in polymer processing. There are several definitions; one is

8. *Answer choices:*

(see index for correct answer)

- a. Ideal chain
- b. Chain shuttling polymerization
- c. Vicat softening point
- d. Equivalent weight

Guidance: level 1

:: Catalysis ::

In chemistry, _____ is catalysis in a solution by a soluble catalyst. _____ refers to catalytic reactions where the catalyst is in the same phase as the reactants. _____ applies to reactions in the gas phase and even in solids. Heterogeneous catalysis is the alternative to _____ , where the catalysis occurs at the interface of two phases, typically gas-solid. The term is used almost exclusively to describe solutions and often implies catalysis by organometallic compounds.

9. *Answer choices:*

(see index for correct answer)

- a. Homogeneous catalysis
- b. Photocatalysis
- c. Cuprospinel
- d. Autocatalytic

Guidance: level 1

:: Enzymes ::

_____ s are enzymes that incorporate one hydroxyl group into substrates in many metabolic pathways. In this reaction, the two atoms of dioxygen are reduced to one hydroxyl group and one H_2O molecule by the concomitant oxidation of NADH. One important subset of the _____ s, the cytochrome P450 omega hydroxylases, is used by cells to metabolize arachidonic acid to the cell signaling molecules, 20-hydroxyeicosatetraenoic acid or to reduce or totally inactivate the activate signaling molecules for example by hydroxylating leukotriene B4 to 20-hydroxy-leukotriene B5, 5-hydroxyeicosatetraenoic acid to 5,20-dihydroxyeicosatetraenoic acid, 5-oxo-eicosatetraenoic acid to 5-oxo-20-hydroxyeicosatetraenoic acid, 12-hydroxyeicosatetraenoic acid to 12,20-dihydroxyeicosatetraenoic acid, and epoxyeicosatrienoic acids to 20-hydroxy-epoxyeicosatrienoic acids.

Exam Probability: **High**

10. *Answer choices:*

(see index for correct answer)

- a. Affinity label
- b. Myrosinase
- c. Monooxygenase
- d. Furin

Guidance: level 1

:: Chemical reactions ::

_____ is a theory that was proposed independently by Max Trautz in 1916 and William Lewis in 1918. The _____ states that when suitable particles of the reactant hit each other, only a certain fraction of the collisions cause any noticeable or significant chemical change; these successful changes are called successful collisions. The successful collisions must have enough energy, also known as activation energy, at the moment of impact to break the pre-existing bonds and form all new bonds. This results in the products of the reaction. Increasing the concentration of the reactant particles or raising the temperature - which brings about more collisions and hence more successful collisions - therefore increases the rate of a reaction.

Exam Probability: **Low**

11. *Answer choices:*

(see index for correct answer)

- a. Auxochrome
- b. Comproportionation
- c. Collision theory
- d. Isomerization

:: Chemical processes ::

A _____ is the rapid combustion of fine particles suspended in the air within an enclosed location. _____ s can occur where any dispersed powdered combustible material is present in high-enough concentrations in the atmosphere or other oxidizing gaseous medium, such as pure oxygen. In cases when fuel plays the role of a combustible material, the explosion is known as a fuel-air explosion.

Exam Probability: **Low**

12. *Answer choices:*

(see index for correct answer)

- a. Dust explosion
- b. Mercury silvering
- c. Cryogenic nitrogen plant
- d. Osmotic dehydration

:: Alchemical processes ::

_____ is a metabolic process that produces chemical changes in organic substrates through the action of enzymes. In biochemistry, it is narrowly defined as the extraction of energy from carbohydrates in the absence of oxygen. In the context of food production, it may more broadly refer to any process in which the activity of microorganisms brings about a desirable change to a foodstuff or beverage. The science of _____ is known as zymology.

Exam Probability: **High**

13. *Answer choices:*

(see index for correct answer)

- a. Ceration
- b. Fermentation in food processing
- c. Projection
- d. Putrefying bacteria

Guidance: level 1

:: Cooling technology ::

In physics, _____ is the production and behaviour of materials at very low temperatures. A person who studies elements that have been subjected to extremely cold temperatures is called a cryogenicist.

Exam Probability: **High**

14. *Answer choices:*

(see index for correct answer)

- a. Outside air economizer
- b. Zero bleed for cooling towers
- c. Discharge pressure
- d. Dilution refrigerator

Guidance: level 1

:: Chemical elements ::

_____ is a chemical element with symbol Cr and atomic number 24. It is the first element in group 6. It is a steely-grey, lustrous, hard and brittle transition metal. _____ is also the main additive in stainless steel, to which it adds anti-corrosive properties. _____ is also highly valued as a metal that is able to be highly polished while resisting tarnishing. Polished _____ reflects almost 70% of the visible spectrum, with almost 90% of infrared light being reflected. The name of the element is derived from the Greek word μα, chroma, meaning color, because many _____ compounds are intensely colored.

Exam Probability: **Low**

15. *Answer choices:*

(see index for correct answer)

- a. Uranium
- b. Chromium

- c. Neptunium
- d. Gallium

Guidance: level 1

:: Heating, ventilating, and air conditioning ::

A _____ is a heat rejection device that rejects waste heat to the atmosphere through the cooling of a water stream to a lower temperature. _____ s may either use the evaporation of water to remove process heat and cool the working fluid to near the wet-bulb air temperature or, in the case of closed circuit dry _____ s, rely solely on air to cool the working fluid to near the dry-bulb air temperature.

Exam Probability: **Medium**

16. *Answer choices:*

(see index for correct answer)

- a. Natural ventilation
- b. Cooling tower
- c. Bell mouth
- d. Deep water source cooling

Guidance: level 1

:: Plasma physics ::

In numerous fields of study, the component of _____ within a system is generally characterized by some of the outputs or internal states growing without bounds. Not all systems that are not stable are unstable; systems can also be marginally stable or exhibit limit cycle behavior.

Exam Probability: **High**

17. *Answer choices:*

(see index for correct answer)

- a. Columbia Non-neutral Torus
- b. Instability
- c. Atmospheric-pressure plasma
- d. Ambipolar diffusion

Guidance: level 1

:: Neurotoxins ::

_____ , also known as methyl alcohol among others, is a chemical with the formula CH3OH . _____ acquired the name wood alcohol because it was once produced chiefly by the destructive distillation of wood. Today, _____ is mainly produced industrially by hydrogenation of carbon monoxide.

Exam Probability: **High**

18. *Answer choices:*

(see index for correct answer)

- a. Aconitum
- b. Discrepin
- c. Methanol
- d. Jingzhaotoxin

Guidance: level 1

:: Chemical reactions ::

_____ s, or more formally, alk _____ s, are a type of reactive structure or intermediate in organic chemistry that is represented as an alkene with a hydroxyl group attached to one end of the alkene double bond. The terms _____ and alk _____ are portmanteaus deriving from "-ene"/"alkene" and the "-ol" suffix indicating the hydroxyl group of alcohols, dropping the terminal "-e" of the first term. Generation of _____ s often involves removal of a hydrogen adjacent to the carbonyl group—i.e., deprotonation, its removal as a proton, H+. When this proton is not returned at the end of the stepwise process, the result is an anion termed an _____ ate . The _____ ate structures shown are schematic; a more modern representation considers the molecular orbitals that are formed and occupied by electrons in the _____ ate. Similarly, generation of the _____ often is accompanied by "trapping" or masking of the hydroxy group as an ether, such as a silyl _____ ether.

Exam Probability: **Medium**

19. *Answer choices:*

(see index for correct answer)

- a. Adduct
- b. Enol
- c. Chemoselectivity
- d. Chemical process of decomposition

Guidance: level 1

:: Physical chemistry ::

In chemistry, a _____ is a special type of homogeneous mixture composed of two or more substances. In such a mixture, a solute is a substance dissolved in another substance, known as a solvent. The mixing process of a _____ happens at a scale where the effects of chemical polarity are involved, resulting in interactions that are specific to solvation. The _____ assumes the phase of the solvent when the solvent is the larger fraction of the mixture, as is commonly the case. The concentration of a solute in a _____ is the mass of that solute expressed as a percentage of the mass of the whole _____ . The term aqueous _____ is when one of the solvents is water.

Exam Probability: **High**

20. *Answer choices:*

(see index for correct answer)

- a. Solution
- b. Kinetic scheme
- c. Hansen solubility parameter
- d. Effusion

:: Alkenyl groups ::

An _____ group is a substituent with the structural formula H2C=CH-CH2R, where R is the rest of the molecule. It consists of a methylene bridge attached to a vinyl group . The name is derived from the Latin word for garlic, Allium sativum. In 1844, Theodor Wertheim isolated an _____ derivative from garlic oil and named it "Schwefel _____ ". The term _____ applies to many compounds related to H2C=CH-CH2, some of which are of practical or of everyday importance, for example, _____ chloride.

Exam Probability: **High**

21. *Answer choices:*

(see index for correct answer)

- a. Crotyl
- b. Allyl

:: Reaction mechanisms ::

_____ is the inversion of a chiral center in a molecule in a chemical reaction. Since a molecule can form two enantiomers around a chiral center, the _____ converts the configuration of the molecule from one enantiomeric form to the other. For example, in an SN2 reaction, _____ occurs at a tetrahedral carbon atom. It can be visualized by imagining an umbrella turned inside-out in a gale. In the _____ , the backside attack by the nucleophile in an SN2 reaction gives rise to a product whose configuration is opposite to the reactant. Therefore, during SN2 reaction, 100% inversion of product takes place. This is known as _____ .

Exam Probability: **Medium**

22. *Answer choices:*

(see index for correct answer)

- a. Bartell mechanism
- b. Allylic rearrangement
- c. ANRORC mechanism
- d. Beta scission

Guidance: level 1

:: Functional groups ::

In organic chemistry an _____ is an alkene with an alkoxy substituent. The general structure is R2C=CR-OR where R = H, alkyl, or aryl. A common subfamily of _____ s are vinyl ethers, with the formula ROCH=CH2. Important _____ s include the reagent 3,4-dihydropyran and the monomers methyl vinyl ether and ethyl vinyl ether.

23. *Answer choices:*

(see index for correct answer)

- a. Sultone
- b. Thioketal
- c. Acyl halide
- d. Urea

Guidance: level 1

:: Chemistry ::

_____ , also called sustainable chemistry, is an area of chemistry and chemical engineering focused on the designing of products and processes that minimize or eliminate the use and generation of hazardous substances. While environmental chemistry focuses on the effects of polluting chemicals on nature, _____ focuses on the environmental impact of chemistry, including technological approaches to preventing pollution and reducing consumption of nonrenewable resources.

Exam Probability: **Low**

24. *Answer choices:*

(see index for correct answer)

- a. DLVO theory

- b. Green chemistry
- c. Cheminformatics
- d. Chemical compound

Guidance: level 1

:: Chemical engineering ::

_____ is a waste treatment process that involves the combustion of organic substances contained in waste materials. _____ and other high-temperature waste treatment systems are described as "thermal treatment". _____ of waste materials converts the waste into ash, flue gas and heat. The ash is mostly formed by the inorganic constituents of the waste and may take the form of solid lumps or particulates carried by the flue gas. The flue gases must be cleaned of gaseous and particulate pollutants before they are dispersed into the atmosphere. In some cases, the heat generated by _____ can be used to generate electric power.

Exam Probability: **Medium**

25. *Answer choices:*
(see index for correct answer)

- a. Institution of Fire Engineers
- b. Relative volatility
- c. Selective catalytic reduction
- d. Air pollutant concentrations

Guidance: level 1

:: Analytical chemistry ::

A _____ is a method that converts a mixture or solution of chemical substances into two or more distinct product mixtures. At least one of results of the separation is enriched in one or more of the source mixture's constituents. In some cases, a separation may fully divide the mixture into pure constituents. Separations exploit differences in chemical properties or physical properties between the constituents of a mixture.

Exam Probability: **Low**

26. *Answer choices:*

(see index for correct answer)

- a. Electron microprobe
- b. Pervaporation
- c. Atomic absorption spectroscopy
- d. Separation process

Guidance: level 1

:: Chemical engineering ::

_____ is a process of removing heat from a low-temperature reservoir and transferring it to a high-temperature reservoir. The work of heat transfer is traditionally driven by mechanical means, but can also be driven by heat, magnetism, electricity, laser, or other means. _____ has many applications, including, but not limited to: household refrigerators, industrial freezers, cryogenics, and air conditioning. Heat pumps may use the heat output of the _____ process, and also may be designed to be reversible, but are otherwise similar to air conditioning units.

Exam Probability: **Low**

27. *Answer choices:*

(see index for correct answer)

- a. Fused quartz
- b. Industrial water treatment
- c. Powder deaerator
- d. Heat transfer

Guidance: level 1

:: Anaerobic digestion ::

_____ is the mixture of gases produced by the breakdown of organic matter in the absence of oxygen. _____ can be produced from raw materials such as agricultural waste, manure, municipal waste, plant material, sewage, green waste or food waste. _____ is a renewable energy source.

28. *Answer choices:*

(see index for correct answer)

- a. Acetogen
- b. Digestate
- c. Biogas
- d. Thermophile

Guidance: level 1

:: Monomers ::

_____ s are the salts, esters, and conjugate bases of acrylic acid and its derivatives. The _____ ion is the anion $CH_2=CHCOO-$. Often _____ refers to esters of acrylic acid, the most common member being methyl _____ . _____ s contain vinyl groups directly attached to the carbonyl carbon. These monomers are of interest because they are bifunctional: the vinyl group is susceptible to polymerization and the carboxylate group carries myriad functionality. Modified _____ s are also numerous, include meth _____ s and cyano _____ s .

29. *Answer choices:*

(see index for correct answer)

- a. Acrylate
- b. Ethyl acrylate
- c. Diphenyl carbonate
- d. Itaconic acid

Guidance: level 1

:: Physical chemistry ::

An _____ is a substance that produces an electrically conducting solution when dissolved in a polar solvent, such as water. The dissolved _____ separates into cations and anions, which disperse uniformly through the solvent. Electrically, such a solution is neutral. If an electric potential is applied to such a solution, the cations of the solution are drawn to the electrode that has an abundance of electrons, while the anions are drawn to the electrode that has a deficit of electrons. The movement of anions and cations in opposite directions within the solution amounts to a current. This includes most soluble salts, acids, and bases. Some gases, such as hydrogen chloride, under conditions of high temperature or low pressure can also function as _____ s. _____ solutions can also result from the dissolution of some biological and synthetic polymers , termed "poly _____ s", which contain charged functional groups. A substance that dissociates into ions in solution acquires the capacity to conduct electricity. Sodium, potassium, chloride, calcium, magnesium, and phosphate are examples of _____ s.

Exam Probability: **High**

30. *Answer choices:*

(see index for correct answer)

- a. Photoelectron photoion coincidence spectroscopy
- b. Electrolyte
- c. DECHEMA model
- d. Colligative properties

Guidance: level 1

:: Name reactions ::

The _____ is a chemical reaction used in organic chemistry for ring formation. It was discovered by Robert Robinson in 1935 as a method to create a six membered ring by forming three new carbon–carbon bonds. The method uses a ketone and a methyl vinyl ketone to form an a,ß-unsaturated ketone in a cyclohexane ring by a Michael addition followed by an aldol condensation. This procedure is one of the key methods to form fused ring systems.

Exam Probability: **Medium**

31. *Answer choices:*
(see index for correct answer)

- a. Ugi reaction
- b. Letts nitrile synthesis
- c. Tishchenko reaction
- d. Robinson annulation

Guidance: level 1

:: Refrigerants ::

_____ is an organic compound with the formula C4H10 that is an alkane with four carbon atoms. _____ is a gas at room temperature and atmospheric pressure. The term may refer to either of two structural isomers, n- _____ or iso _____ , or to a mixture of these isomers. In the IUPAC nomenclature, however, " _____ " refers only to the n- _____ isomer. _____ s are highly flammable, colorless, easily liquefied gases that quickly vaporize at room temperature. The name _____ comes from the roots but- and -ane. It was discovered by the chemist Edward Frankland in 1849. It was found dissolved in crude petroleum in 1864 by Edmund Ronalds, who was the first to describe its properties.

Exam Probability: **Low**

32. *Answer choices:*

(see index for correct answer)

- a. Hydrofluoroolefin
- b. R-406A
- c. 1,1,1,2-Tetrafluoroethane
- d. Butane

Guidance: level 1

:: Cycloalkanes ::

_____ is a cycloalkane with the molecular formula C6H12. _____ is a colourless, flammable liquid with a distinctive detergent-like odor, reminiscent of cleaning products . _____ is mainly used for the industrial production of adipic acid and caprolactam, which are precursors to nylon.

Exam Probability: **Medium**

33. *Answer choices:*

(see index for correct answer)

- a. Cycloalkane
- b. Cycloheptane
- c. Cyclotetradecane
- d. Cyclohexane

Guidance: level 1

:: Inorganic amines ::

_____ is a compound of nitrogen and hydrogen with the formula NH3. The simplest pnictogen hydride, _____ is a colourless gas with a characteristic pungent smell. It is a common nitrogenous waste, particularly among aquatic organisms, and it contributes significantly to the nutritional needs of terrestrial organisms by serving as a precursor to food and fertilizers. _____ , either directly or indirectly, is also a building block for the synthesis of many pharmaceutical products and is used in many commercial cleaning products. It is mainly collected by downward displacement of both air and water. _____ is named for the _____ ns, worshipers of the Egyptian god Amun, who used ammonium chloride in their rituals.

Exam Probability: **Medium**

34. *Answer choices:*

(see index for correct answer)

- a. Nitrogen triiodide
- b. Hydroxylamine
- c. Ammonia
- d. Nitrogen trifluoride

Guidance: level 1

:: Zwitterions ::

_____ s are organic compounds containing amine and carboxyl functional groups, along with a side chain specific to each _____ . The key elements of an _____ are carbon , hydrogen , oxygen , and nitrogen , although other elements are found in the side chains of certain _____ s. About 500 naturally occurring _____ s are known and can be classified in many ways. They can be classified according to the core structural functional groups' locations as alpha- , beta- , gamma- or delta- _____ s; other categories relate to polarity, pH level, and side chain group type . In the form of proteins, _____ residues form the second-largest component of human muscles and other tissues. Beyond their role as residues in proteins, _____ s participate in a number of processes such as neurotransmitter transport and biosynthesis.

Exam Probability: **High**

35. *Answer choices:*

(see index for correct answer)

- a. Perifosine
- b. Cephaloridine
- c. Edelfosine
- d. Amino acid

Guidance: level 1

:: Catalysis ::

_____ refers to the use of living, also called enzymes systems or their parts to speed up chemical reactions. In biocatalytic processes, natural catalysts, such as enzymes, perform chemical transformations on organic compounds. Both enzymes that have been more or less isolated and enzymes still residing inside living cells are employed for this task.. The modern usage of biotechnologically produced and possibly modified enzymes for organic synthesis is termed chemoenzymatic synthesis; the reactions performed are chemoenzymatic reactions.

Exam Probability: **Low**

36. *Answer choices:*

(see index for correct answer)

- a. Biocatalysis
- b. Electrocatalyst
- c. Catalyst poisoning
- d. Catalytic cycle

Guidance: level 1

:: Chemical engineering ::

_____ s are heat exchangers typically used to provide heat to the bottom of industrial distillation columns. They boil the liquid from the bottom of a distillation column to generate vapors which are returned to the column to drive the distillation separation. The heat supplied to the column by the _____ at the bottom of the column is removed by the condenser at the top of the column.

37. *Answer choices:*

(see index for correct answer)

- a. Rotating biological contactor
- b. Flange
- c. Downstream processing
- d. Nucleic acid thermodynamics

Guidance: level 1

:: Catalysis ::

The _____ reaction is an enantioselective chemical reaction to prepare 2,3-epoxyalcohols from primary and secondary allylic alcohols.

38. *Answer choices:*

(see index for correct answer)

- a. Wilhelm Normann
- b. Sharpless epoxidation
- c. Catalytically perfect enzyme
- d. Sabatier principle

:: Environmental engineering ::

_____ is a technology and applied science using engineering, chemistry, and other sciences involving the mechanical properties and use of liquids. At a very basic level, _____ is the liquid counterpart of pneumatics, which concerns gases. Fluid mechanics provides the theoretical foundation for _____ , which focuses on the applied engineering using the properties of fluids. In its fluid power applications, _____ is used for the generation, control, and transmission of power by the use of pressurized liquids. Hydraulic topics range through some parts of science and most of engineering modules, and cover concepts such as pipe flow, dam design, fluidics and fluid control circuitry. The principles of _____ are in use naturally in the human body within the vascular system and erectile tissue. Free surface _____ is the branch of _____ dealing with free surface flow, such as occurring in rivers, canals, lakes, estuaries and seas. Its sub-field open-channel flow studies the flow in open channels.

Exam Probability: **High**

39. *Answer choices:*

(see index for correct answer)

- a. Ecological engineering
- b. National Environmental Engineering Research Institute
- c. Hurricane engineering
- d. Hydraulics

:: Convection ::

The _____ is the mass transfer along an interface between two fluids due to a gradient of the surface tension. In the case of temperature dependence, this phenomenon may be called thermo-capillary convection .

Exam Probability: **Medium**

40. *Answer choices:*

(see index for correct answer)

- a. Marangoni effect
- b. Urban thermal plume
- c. Convection microwave
- d. Rayleigh number

Guidance: level 1

:: Posttranslational modification ::

A _____ is an enzyme that helps proteolysis: protein catabolism by hydrolysis of peptide bonds. _____ s have evolved multiple times, and different classes of _____ can perform the same reaction by completely different catalytic mechanisms. _____ s can be found in all forms of life and viruses.

41. *Answer choices:*

(see index for correct answer)

- a. Protease
- b. Alagebrium
- c. Hyperphosphorylation
- d. Phosphorylation

Guidance: level 1

:: Physical chemistry ::

In thermodynamics, _____ of a species is energy that can be absorbed or released due to a change of the particle number of the given species, e.g. in a chemical reaction or phase transition. The _____ of a species in a mixture is defined as the rate of change of free energy of a thermodynamic system with respect to the change in the number of atoms or molecules of the species that are added to the system. Thus, it is the partial derivative of the free energy with respect to the amount of the species, all other species` concentrations in the mixture remaining constant. The molar _____ is also known as partial molar free energy. When both temperature and pressure are held constant, _____ is the partial molar Gibbs free energy. At chemical equilibrium or in phase equilibrium the total sum of the product of _____ s and stoichiometric coefficients is zero, as the free energy is at a minimum.

Exam Probability: **Medium**

42. *Answer choices:*

- a. Electron transfer
- b. Opacifier
- c. Steric factor
- d. Chemical potential

Guidance: level 1

:: Chemical processes ::

_____ is a separation process in which a certain quantity of a mixture is divided during a phase transition, into a number of smaller quantities in which the composition varies according to a gradient. Fractions are collected based on differences in a specific property of the individual components. A common trait in _____ s is the need to find an optimum between the amount of fractions collected and the desired purity in each fraction. _____ makes it possible to isolate more than two components in a mixture in a single run. This property sets it apart from other separation techniques.

Exam Probability: **High**

43. *Answer choices:*

- a. Black oxide
- b. Fractionation

- c. Cumene process
- d. Solvay process

Guidance: level 1

:: Polymers ::

A _____ is a large molecule, or macromolecule, composed of many repeated subunits. Due to their broad range of properties, both synthetic and natural _____ s play essential and ubiquitous roles in everyday life. _____ s range from familiar synthetic plastics such as polystyrene to natural bio _____ s such as DNA and proteins that are fundamental to biological structure and function. _____ s, both natural and synthetic, are created via _____ ization of many small molecules, known as monomers. Their consequently large molecular mass relative to small molecule compounds produces unique physical properties, including toughness, viscoelasticity, and a tendency to form glasses and semicrystalline structures rather than crystals. The terms _____ and resin are often synonymous with plastic.

Exam Probability: **High**

44. *Answer choices:*

(see index for correct answer)

- a. Polyanhydrides
- b. Arabinogalactan
- c. Syrup
- d. Polymer

:: Analytical chemistry ::

_____ is an exchange of ions between two electrolytes or between an electrolyte solution and a complex. In most cases the term is used to denote the processes of purification, separation, and decontamination of aqueous and other ion-containing solutions with solid polymeric or mineralic " _____ rs".

Exam Probability: **High**

45. *Answer choices:*

(see index for correct answer)

- a. atomic absorption
- b. Ion exchange
- c. Colorimetric analysis
- d. Water content

:: Light-sensitive chemicals ::

_____ is a chemical compound with the formula H2O2. In its pure form, it is a pale blue, clear liquid, slightly more viscous than water. _____ is the simplest peroxide . It is used as an oxidizer, bleaching agent and antiseptic. Concentrated _____ , or "high-test peroxide", is a reactive oxygen species and has been used as a propellant in rocketry. Its chemistry is dominated by the nature of its unstable peroxide bond.

Exam Probability: **Low**

46. *Answer choices:*

(see index for correct answer)

- a. Hydrogen peroxide
- b. Psilocybin
- c. Ammonium dichromate
- d. Potassium dichromate

Guidance: level 1

:: Functional groups ::

An _____ is a cyclic ether with a three-atom ring. This ring approximates an equilateral triangle, which makes it strained, and hence highly reactive, more so than other ethers. They are produced on a large scale for many applications. In general, low molecular weight _____ s are colourless and nonpolar, and often volatile.

Exam Probability: **Low**

47. *Answer choices:*

(see index for correct answer)

- a. Epoxide
- b. Acyl azide
- c. Alkene
- d. Tosylhydrazone

Guidance: level 1

:: Amines ::

_____ is an organic chemical compound with the condensed structural formula C6H5CH2NH2 . It consists of a benzyl group, C6H5CH2, attached to an amine functional group, NH2. This colorless liquid is a common precursor in organic synthesis and used in the industrial production of many pharmaceuticals. The hydrochloride salt was used to treat motion sickness on the Mercury-Atlas 6 mission in which NASA astronaut John Glenn became the first American to orbit the Earth.

Exam Probability: **High**

48. *Answer choices:*

(see index for correct answer)

- a. Protriptyline
- b. EDDS
- c. Benzylamine

- d. Cycloalkylamine

Guidance: level 1

:: Catalysis ::

_____ s are macromolecular biological catalysts. _____ s accelerate chemical reactions. The molecules upon which _____ s may act are called substrates and the _____ converts the substrates into different molecules known as products. Almost all metabolic processes in the cell need _____ catalysis in order to occur at rates fast enough to sustain life. Metabolic pathways depend upon _____ s to catalyze individual steps. The study of _____ s is called enzymology and a new field of pseudo _____ analysis has recently grown up, recognising that during evolution, some _____ s have lost the ability to carry out biological catalysis, which is often reflected in their amino acid sequences and unusual `pseudocatalytic` properties.

Exam Probability: **Low**

49. *Answer choices:*
(see index for correct answer)

- a. Photofermentation
- b. Asymmetric ion-pairing catalysis
- c. Enzyme
- d. Catalysis

Guidance: level 1

:: Fluid mechanics ::

A _____ is a device designed to control the direction or characteristics of a fluid flow as it exits an enclosed chamber or pipe.

Exam Probability: **Low**

50. *Answer choices:*

(see index for correct answer)

- a. Cheng rotation vane
- b. Perfect fluid
- c. Pipe flow
- d. Nozzle

Guidance: level 1

:: Chemical processes ::

_____ is the adhesion of atoms, ions or molecules from a gas, liquid or dissolved solid to a surface. This process creates a film of the adsorbate on the surface of the adsorbent. This process differs from absorption, in which a fluid is dissolved by or permeates a liquid or solid , respectively.
_____ is a surface phenomenon, while absorption involves the whole volume of the material. The term sorption encompasses both processes, while desorption is the reverse of it.

51. *Answer choices:*

(see index for correct answer)

- a. Autocatalysis
- b. Aludel
- c. Adsorption
- d. Cathodic protection

Guidance: level 1

:: Condensed matter physics ::

A _____ is any substance at a temperature and pressure above its critical point, where distinct liquid and gas phases do not exist. It can effuse through solids like a gas, and dissolve materials like a liquid. In addition, close to the critical point, small changes in pressure or temperature result in large changes in density, allowing many properties of a _____ to be "fine-tuned".

Exam Probability: **Medium**

52. *Answer choices:*

(see index for correct answer)

- a. Strong confinement limit
- b. Computational chemical methods in solid-state physics

- c. Hall effect
- d. Supercritical fluid

Guidance: level 1

:: Metallurgical processes ::

_____ companies are companies that specialize in combining raw materials such as polyesters, adhesives, silicone, adhesive tapes, foams, plastics, felts, rubbers, liners and metals, as well as other materials, to create new products.

Exam Probability: **Low**

53. *Answer choices:*

(see index for correct answer)

- a. Hydrogen analyzer
- b. Diffusion hardening
- c. Lancashire hearth
- d. Converting

Guidance: level 1

:: Teratogens ::

_____ is an organic chemical compound with the chemical formula C6H6. The _____ molecule is composed of six carbon atoms joined in a ring with one hydrogen atom attached to each. As it contains only carbon and hydrogen atoms, _____ is classed as a hydrocarbon.

Exam Probability: **High**

54. *Answer choices:*

(see index for correct answer)

- a. Diethylstilbestrol
- b. Benzene
- c. Agent Orange
- d. N-Nitroso-N-methylurea

Guidance: level 1

:: Monomers ::

_____ , also known as ethenylbenzene, vinylbenzene, and phenylethene, is an organic compound with the chemical formula C6H5CH=CH2. This derivative of benzene is a colorless oily liquid that evaporates easily and has a sweet smell, although high concentrations have a less pleasant odor. _____ is the precursor to poly _____ and several copolymers. Approximately 25 million tonnes of _____ were produced in 2010.

Exam Probability: **High**

55. *Answer choices:*

(see index for correct answer)

- a. Styrene
- b. Adipic acid
- c. Cyclobutene
- d. Vinyl chloride

Guidance: level 1

:: Condensed matter physics ::

The _____ is the angle, conventionally measured through the liquid, where a liquid–vapor interface meets a solid surface. It quantifies the wettability of a solid surface by a liquid via the Young equation. A given system of solid, liquid, and vapor at a given temperature and pressure has a unique equilibrium _____ . However, in practice a dynamic phenomenon of _____ hysteresis is often observed, ranging from the advancing _____ to the receding _____ . The equilibrium contact is within those values, and can be calculated from them. The equilibrium _____ reflects the relative strength of the liquid, solid, and vapor molecular interaction.

Exam Probability: **Low**

56. *Answer choices:*

(see index for correct answer)

- a. Coercivity
- b. Contact angle

- c. Kondo effect
- d. Degenerate matter

Guidance: level 1

:: Alkenes ::

_____ is a medication used to treat malaria and babesiosis. This includes the treatment of malaria due to Plasmodium falciparum that is resistant to chloroquine when artesunate is not available. While used for restless legs syndrome, it is not recommended for this purpose due to the risk of side effects. It can be taken by mouth or used intravenously. Malaria resistance to _____ occurs in certain areas of the world. _____ is also the ingredient in tonic water that gives it its bitter taste.

Exam Probability: **Medium**

57. *Answer choices:*

(see index for correct answer)

- a. Nerolidol
- b. Quinine
- c. Prenol
- d. Thujene

Guidance: level 1

:: Heat transfer ::

_____ is the heat transfer due to the bulk movement of molecules within fluids such as gases and liquids, including molten rock . _____ includes sub-mechanisms of advection , and diffusion .

Exam Probability: **High**

58. *Answer choices:*

(see index for correct answer)

- a. Emissivity
- b. Thermal expansion
- c. Convection
- d. Applied Thermal Engineering

Guidance: level 1

:: Anaerobic digestion ::

_____ is a chemical compound with the chemical formula CH_4 . It is a group-14 hydride and the simplest alkane, and is the main constituent of natural gas. The relative abundance of _____ on Earth makes it an attractive fuel, although capturing and storing it poses challenges due to its gaseous state under normal conditions for temperature and pressure.

Exam Probability: **Low**

59. *Answer choices:*

(see index for correct answer)

- a. Thermophile
- b. Acidogenesis
- c. Methane
- d. Decomposition

Guidance: level 1

Inorganic chemistry

Inorganic chemistry deals with the synthesis and behavior of inorganic and organometallic compounds. This field covers all chemical compounds except the myriad organic compounds (carbon based compounds, usually containing C-H bonds), which are the subjects of organic chemistry. The distinction between the two disciplines is far from absolute, as there is much overlap in the subdiscipline of organometallic chemistry. It has applications in every aspect of the chemical industry, including catalysis, materials science, pigments, surfactants, coatings, medications, fuels, and agriculture.

:: Chemical elements ::

_____ is a chemical element with symbol F and atomic number 9. It is the lightest halogen and exists as a highly toxic pale yellow diatomic gas at standard conditions. As the most electronegative element, it is extremely reactive, as it reacts with almost all other elements, except for helium and neon.

Exam Probability: **High**

1. *Answer choices:*

(see index for correct answer)

- a. Fluorine
- b. Neptunium
- c. Thorium
- d. Lead

Guidance: level 1

:: Physical quantities ::

A _____ is any property that is measurable, whose value describes a state of a physical system. The changes in the physical properties of a system can be used to describe its changes between momentary states. Physical properties are often referred to as observables. They are not modal properties. Quantifiable _____ is called physical quantity.

Exam Probability: **Low**

2. *Answer choices:*

(see index for correct answer)

- a. Density
- b. Physical properties
- c. Physical property
- d. Specific gravity

:: Chemical elements ::

_____ is a chemical element with symbol Ga and atomic number 31. Elemental _____ is a soft, silvery blue metal at standard temperature and pressure; however in its liquid state it becomes silvery white. If too much force is applied _____ may fracture conchoidally. It is in group 13 of the periodic table, and thus has similarities to the other metals of the group, aluminium, indium, and thallium. _____ does not occur as a free element in nature, but as _____ compounds in trace amounts in zinc ores and in bauxite. Elemental _____ is a liquid at temperatures greater than 29.76 °C , above room temperature, but below the normal human body temperature of 37 °C . Hence, the metal will melt in a person's hands.

Exam Probability: **Low**

3. *Answer choices:*

(see index for correct answer)

- a. Plutonium
- b. Ununseptium
- c. Polonium
- d. Gallium

:: Bases ::

A Lewis acid is a chemical species that contains an empty orbital which is capable of accepting an electron pair from a _____ to form a Lewis adduct. A _____ , then, is any species that has a filled orbital containing an electron pair which is not involved in bonding but may form a dative bond with a Lewis acid to form a Lewis adduct. For example, NH3 is a _____ , because it can donate its lone pair of electrons. Trimethylborane is a Lewis acid as it is capable of accepting a lone pair. In a Lewis adduct, the Lewis acid and base share an electron pair furnished by the _____ , forming a dative bond. In the context of a specific chemical reaction between NH3 and Me3B, the lone pair from NH3 will form a dative bond with the empty orbital of Me3B to form an adduct NH3•BMe3. The terminology refers to the contributions of Gilbert N. Lewis.

Exam Probability: **Medium**

4. *Answer choices:*

(see index for correct answer)

- a. Saponification
- b. Lewis base
- c. Soluene
- d. Lyate ion

Guidance: level 1

:: Metals ::

_____ is a type of chemical bonding that rises from the electrostatic attractive force between conduction electrons and positively charged metal ions. It may be described as the sharing of free electrons among a structure of positively charged ions . _____ accounts for many physical properties of metals, such as strength, ductility, thermal and electrical resistivity and conductivity, opacity, and luster.

Exam Probability: **Low**

5. *Answer choices:*

(see index for correct answer)

- a. Alonizing
- b. Light metal
- c. Non-ferrous metal
- d. Metallic bonding

Guidance: level 1

:: Electrochemical equations ::

In electrochemistry, the _____ is an equation that relates the reduction potential of an electrochemical reaction to the standard electrode potential, temperature, and activities of the chemical species undergoing reduction and oxidation. It was named after Walther Nernst, a German physical chemist who formulated the equation.

Exam Probability: **Medium**

6. *Answer choices:*

(see index for correct answer)

- a. Nernst equation
- b. Tafel equation
- c. Cottrell equation

Guidance: level 1

:: Phosphorus oxoacids ::

_____ , is the compound described by the formula H3PO3. This acid is diprotic , not triprotic as might be suggested by this formula. _____ is an intermediate in the preparation of other phosphorus compounds. Organic derivatives of _____ , compounds with the formula RPO3H2, are called phosphonic acids.

Exam Probability: **Low**

7. *Answer choices:*

(see index for correct answer)

- a. Phosphorus acid
- b. Hypophosphorous acid
- c. Triphosphoric acid
- d. Phosphorous acid

:: Mineral acids ::

_____ is a mixture of nitric acid and hydrochloric acid, optimally in a molar ratio of 1:3. _____ is a yellow-orange fuming liquid, so named by alchemists because it can dissolve the noble metals gold and platinum, though not all metals.

Exam Probability: **Low**

8. *Answer choices:*

(see index for correct answer)

- a. Chloric acid
- b. Fluoroantimonic acid
- c. Boric acid
- d. Aqua regia

:: Chemical bonding ::

A _____ in chemistry is a chemical bond between two atoms involving six bonding electrons instead of the usual two in a covalent single bond. The most common _____ , that between two carbon atoms, can be found in alkynes. Other functional groups containing a _____ are cyanides and isocyanides. Some diatomic molecules, such as dinitrogen and carbon monoxide, are also _____ ed. In skeletal formula the _____ is drawn as three parallel lines between the two connected atoms.

Exam Probability: **Low**

9. *Answer choices:*

- a. Triple bond
- b. Formal charge
- c. Double bond
- d. Lewis structure

Guidance: level 1

:: Metalloproteins ::

_____ is an oligomeric protein responsible for oxygen transport in the marine invertebrate phyla of sipunculids, priapulids, brachiopods, and in a single annelid worm genus, Magelona. Myo _____ is a monomeric O2-binding protein found in the muscles of marine invertebrates. _____ and myo _____ are essentially colorless when deoxygenated, but turn a violet-pink in the oxygenated state.

10. *Answer choices:*

(see index for correct answer)

- a. DMSO reductase
- b. Hemerythrin
- c. Superoxide dismutase
- d. Sulfite oxidase

Guidance: level 1

:: Inorganic chemistry ::

_____ is a model that describes the breaking of degeneracies of electron orbital states, usually d or f orbitals, due to a static electric field produced by a surrounding charge distribution . This theory has been used to describe various spectroscopies of transition metal coordination complexes, in particular optical spectra . CFT successfully accounts for some magnetic properties, colors, hydration enthalpies, and spinel structures of transition metal complexes, but it does not attempt to describe bonding. CFT was developed by physicists Hans Bethe and John Hasbrouck van Vleck in the 1930s. CFT was subsequently combined with molecular orbital theory to form the more realistic and complex ligand field theory , which delivers insight into the process of chemical bonding in transition metal complexes.

11. *Answer choices:*

- a. Dihydrogen complex
- b. Crystal field theory
- c. Homoleptic
- d. Inner sphere complex

Guidance: level 1

:: Limestone ::

_____ is the most common type of cement in general use around the world as a basic ingredient of concrete, mortar, stucco, and non-specialty grout. It was developed from other types of hydraulic lime in England in the mid 19th century, and usually originates from limestone. It is a fine powder, produced by heating limestone and clay minerals in a kiln to form clinker, grinding the clinker, and adding 2 to 3 percent of gypsum. Several types of _____ are available. The most common, called ordinary _____ , is grey, but white _____ is also available. Its name is derived from its similarity to Portland stone which was quarried on the Isle of Portland in Dorset, England. It was named by Joseph Aspdin who obtained a patent for it in 1824. However, his son William Aspdin is regarded as the inventor of "modern" _____ due to his developments in the 1840s.

Exam Probability: **Low**

12. *Answer choices:*

- a. Cotham Marble

- b. Ashford Black Marble
- c. Portland Grove Whitbed
- d. Portland cement

Guidance: level 1

:: Minerals ::

A _____ is, broadly speaking, a solid chemical compound that occurs naturally in pure form. A rock may consist of a single _____ , or may be an aggregate of two or more different _____ s, spacially segregated into distinct phases. Compounds that occur only in living beings are usually excluded, but some _____ s are often biogenic and/or are organic compounds in the sense of chemistry . Moreover, living beings often synthesize inorganic _____ s that also occur in rocks.

Exam Probability: **Medium**

13. *Answer choices:*

(see index for correct answer)

- a. Nodule
- b. Mineral
- c. Maskelynite
- d. Wood Opal

Guidance: level 1

:: Electrolysis ::

In chemistry and manufacturing, _____ is a technique that uses a direct electric current to drive an otherwise non-spontaneous chemical reaction. _____ is commercially important as a stage in the separation of elements from naturally occurring sources such as ores using an electrolytic cell. The voltage that is needed for _____ to occur is called the decomposition potential.

Exam Probability: **High**

14. *Answer choices:*

(see index for correct answer)

- a. Kolbe electrolysis
- b. Electrolysis
- c. Hydrion
- d. Patterson Power Cell

Guidance: level 1

:: Electrochemistry ::

A _____ of an element is a summary of the standard electrode potential data of that element. This type of diagram is named after Wendell Mitchell Latimer, an American chemist.

15. *Answer choices:*

(see index for correct answer)

- a. Asian Conference on Electrochemical Power Sources
- b. electroosmotic flow
- c. Galvani potential
- d. Latimer diagram

Guidance: level 1

:: Zwitterions ::

_____ s are organic compounds containing amine and carboxyl functional groups, along with a side chain specific to each _____ . The key elements of an _____ are carbon , hydrogen , oxygen , and nitrogen , although other elements are found in the side chains of certain _____ s. About 500 naturally occurring _____ s are known and can be classified in many ways. They can be classified according to the core structural functional groups` locations as alpha- , beta- , gamma- or delta- _____ s; other categories relate to polarity, pH level, and side chain group type . In the form of proteins, _____ residues form the second-largest component of human muscles and other tissues. Beyond their role as residues in proteins, _____ s participate in a number of processes such as neurotransmitter transport and biosynthesis.

16. *Answer choices:*

(see index for correct answer)

- a. Ceftazidime
- b. Edelfosine
- c. Amino acid
- d. Cephaloridine

Guidance: level 1

:: Chlorides ::

_____ is a metal halide salt composed of potassium and chlorine. It is odorless and has a white or colorless vitreous crystal appearance. The solid dissolves readily in water and its solutions have a salt-like taste. KCl is used as a fertilizer, in medicine, in scientific applications, and in food processing, where it may be known as E number additive E508.

Exam Probability: **Low**

17. *Answer choices:*

(see index for correct answer)

- a. Potassium tetrachloroplatinate
- b. Pararosaniline
- c. Doxacurium chloride
- d. Xenon dichloride

:: Chemical elements ::

_____ is a chemical element with symbol I and atomic number 53. The heaviest of the stable halogens, it exists as a lustrous, purple-black non-metallic solid at standard conditions that melts to form a deep violet liquid at 114 degrees Celsius, and boils to a violet gas at 184 degrees Celsius. The element was discovered by the French chemist Bernard Courtois in 1811. It was named two years later by Joseph Louis Gay-Lussac from this property, after the Greek d "violet-coloured".

Exam Probability: **High**

18. *Answer choices:*

(see index for correct answer)

- a. Iodine
- b. Lanthanum
- c. Unbihexium
- d. Indium

:: Chemical engineering ::

The _____ or rate of reaction is the speed at which reactants are converted into products. For example, the oxidative rusting of iron under Earth's atmosphere is a slow reaction that can take many years, but the combustion of cellulose in a fire is a reaction that takes place in fractions of a second. For most reactions, the rate decreases as the reaction proceeds.

Exam Probability: Medium

19. *Answer choices:*

(see index for correct answer)

- a. Chemical process modeling
- b. Cryo-adsorption
- c. Reaction rate
- d. Industrial water treatment

Guidance: level 1

:: Acetylides ::

_____ refers to chemical compounds with the chemical formulas $MC=CH$ and $MC=CM$, where M is a metal. The term is used loosely and can refer to substituted _____ s having the general structure $RC=CM$. _____ s are reagents in organic synthesis. The calcium _____ commonly called calcium carbide is a major compound of commerce.

Exam Probability: High

20. *Answer choices:*

(see index for correct answer)

- a. Dichloroacetylene
- b. Acetylide
- c. Lithium carbide
- d. Calcium carbide

Guidance: level 1

:: Chemical processes ::

The _____ or ammonia-soda process is the major industrial process for the production of sodium carbonate . The ammonia-soda process was developed into its modern form by Ernest Solvay during the 1860s. The ingredients for this are readily available and inexpensive: salt brine and limestone . The worldwide production of soda ash in 2005 has been estimated at 42 million metric tons, which is more than six kilograms per year for each person on Earth. Solvay-based chemical plants now produce roughly three-quarters of this supply, with the remainder being mined from natural deposits. This method superseded the Leblanc process.

Exam Probability: **Medium**

21. *Answer choices:*

(see index for correct answer)

- a. Disproportionation
- b. Solvay process

- c. Amine gas treating
- d. Ketazine process

Guidance: level 1

:: Free radicals ::

_____ is a colorless gas with the formula NO. It is one of the principal oxides of nitrogen. _____ is a free radical, i.e., it has an unpaired electron, which is sometimes denoted by a dot in its chemical formula, i.e., ·NO. _____ is also a heteronuclear diatomic molecule, a historic class that drew researches which spawned early modern theories of chemical bonding.

Exam Probability: **Low**

22. *Answer choices:*

(see index for correct answer)

- a. N-philes
- b. 5-Dehydro-m-xylylene
- c. Octatetraynyl radical
- d. Nitric oxide

Guidance: level 1

:: Chemical bonding ::

In chemistry, Molecular orbital theory is a method for describing the electronic structure of molecules using quantum mechanics. Electrons are not assigned to individual bonds between atoms, but are treated as moving under the influence of the nuclei in the whole molecule. The spatial and energetic properties of electrons are described by quantum mechanics as molecular orbitals surround two or more atoms in a molecule and contain valence electrons between atoms. Molecular _____ , which was proposed in the early twentieth century, revolutionized the study of bonding by approximating the states of bonded electrons—the molecular orbitals—as linear combinations of atomic orbitals . These approximations are now made by applying the density functional theory or Hartree–Fock models to the Schrödinger equation.

Exam Probability: **Medium**

23. *Answer choices:*

(see index for correct answer)

- a. Orbital theory
- b. Electronegativity
- c. Formal charge
- d. Triple bond

Guidance: level 1

_____

:: Atomic physics ::

In quantum mechanics, the _____ is one of four quantum numbers which are assigned to all electrons in an atom to describe that electron's state. As a discrete variable, the _____ is always an integer. As n increases, the number of electronic shells increases and the electron spends more time farther from the nucleus. As n increases, the electron is also at a higher energy and is, therefore, less tightly bound to the nucleus. The total energy of an electron, as described below, is a negative inverse quadratic function of the _____ n.

Exam Probability: **High**

24. *Answer choices:*

(see index for correct answer)

- a. Auger effect
- b. Principal quantum number
- c. Atomic recoil
- d. Associated Legendre polynomials

Guidance: level 1

:: Equilibrium chemistry ::

_____ or haemoglobin , abbreviated Hb or Hgb, is the iron-containing oxygen-transport metalloprotein in the red blood cells of almost all vertebrates as well as the tissues of some invertebrates. Haemoglobin in blood carries oxygen from the lungs or gills to the rest of the body . There it releases the oxygen to permit aerobic respiration to provide energy to power the functions of the organism in the process called metabolism. A healthy individual has 12 to 20 grams of haemoglobin in every 100 ml of blood.

Exam Probability: **High**

25. *Answer choices:*

(see index for correct answer)

- a. Multimedia fugacity model
- b. Fugacity capacity
- c. Hemoglobin
- d. Specific ion interaction theory

Guidance: level 1

:: Carbonyl complexes ::

_____ s are coordination complexes of transition metals with carbon monoxide ligands. _____ s are useful in organic synthesis and as catalysts or catalyst precursors in homogeneous catalysis, such as hydroformylation and Reppe chemistry. In the Mond process, nickel tetracarbonyl is used to produce pure nickel. In organometallic chemistry, _____ s serve as precursors for the preparation of other organometalic complexes.

26. *Answer choices:*

(see index for correct answer)

- a. Tetrairidium dodecacarbonyl
- b. Dimanganese decacarbonyl
- c. Metal carbonyl
- d. Metallacarboxylic acid

Guidance: level 1

:: Ammine complexes ::

_____ is a chemotherapy medication used to treat a number of cancers. These include testicular cancer, ovarian cancer, cervical cancer, breast cancer, bladder cancer, head and neck cancer, esophageal cancer, lung cancer, mesothelioma, brain tumors and neuroblastoma. It is given by injection into a vein.

Exam Probability: **Low**

27. *Answer choices:*

(see index for correct answer)

- a. Oxaliplatin
- b. Metal ammine complex

- c. Cisplatin

Guidance: level 1

:: Stereochemistry ::

In chemistry, orbital hybridisation is the concept of mixing atomic orbitals into new _____ suitable for the pairing of electrons to form chemical bonds in valence bond theory. _____ are very useful in the explanation of molecular geometry and atomic bonding properties and are symmetrically disposed in space. Although sometimes taught together with the valence shell electron-pair repulsion theory, valence bond and hybridisation are in fact not related to the VSEPR model.

Exam Probability: **Low**

28. *Answer choices:*

(see index for correct answer)

- a. Newman projection
- b. Enantiomer self-disproportionation
- c. Homometric structures
- d. Hybrid orbitals

Guidance: level 1

:: Iron-sulfur proteins ::

_____s are iron–sulfur proteins that mediate electron transfer in a range of metabolic reactions. The term " _____ " was coined by D.C. Wharton of the DuPont Co. and applied to the "iron protein" first purified in 1962 by Mortenson, Valentine, and Carnahan from the anaerobic bacterium Clostridium pasteurianum.

Exam Probability: **Low**

29. *Answer choices:*

(see index for correct answer)

- a. Nitrogenase
- b. Ferredoxin
- c. Iron-sulfur protein
- d. Rieske protein

Guidance: level 1

:: Organoboron compounds ::

_____s are electron-delocalized clusters composed of boron, carbon and hydrogen atoms that may also contain other metallic and nonmetallic elements in the cluster framework. Like many of the related boron hydrides, these clusters are polyhedra or fragments of polyhedra, and are similarly classified as closo-, nido-, arachno-, hypho-, etc. based on whether they represent a complete polyhedron, or a polyhedron that is missing one , two , three , or more vertices. _____s are a notable example of heteroboranes.

30. *Answer choices:*

(see index for correct answer)

- a. BODIPY
- b. -2-Methyl-CBS-oxazaborolidine
- c. Organotrifluoroborate
- d. 2-Aminoethoxydiphenyl borate

Guidance: level 1

:: Chemical element groups ::

A block of the periodic table is a set of chemical elements predominantly characterised by having their highest energy electrons in the same atomic orbital type. The term appears to have been first used by Charles Janet. Each block is named after its characteristic orbital; thus, the blocks are.

Exam Probability: **Medium**

31. *Answer choices:*

(see index for correct answer)

- a. Group
- b. Actinide
- c. Chalcogen

- d. Main group element

Guidance: level 1

:: Chemical elements ::

_____ is a chemical element with symbol P and atomic number 15. Elemental _____ exists in two major forms, white _____ and red _____ , but because it is highly reactive, _____ is never found as a free element on Earth. It has a concentration in the Earth's crust of about one gram per kilogram . With few exceptions, minerals containing _____ are in the maximally oxidized state as inorganic phosphate rocks.

Exam Probability: **High**

32. *Answer choices:*
(see index for correct answer)

- a. Beryllium
- b. Nitrogen
- c. Hassium
- d. Mercury

Guidance: level 1

:: Chemical elements ::

_____ is a chemical element with symbol Zr and atomic number 40. The name _____ is taken from the name of the mineral zircon , the most important source of _____ . It is a lustrous, grey-white, strong transition metal that closely resembles hafnium and, to a lesser extent, titanium. _____ is mainly used as a refractory and opacifier, although small amounts are used as an alloying agent for its strong resistance to corrosion. _____ forms a variety of inorganic and organometallic compounds such as _____ dioxide and zirconocene dichloride, respectively. Five isotopes occur naturally, three of which are stable. _____ compounds have no known biological role.

Exam Probability: **Low**

33. *Answer choices:*

(see index for correct answer)

- a. Polonium
- b. Roentgenium
- c. Zinc
- d. Zirconium

Guidance: level 1

:: Inorganic chemistry ::

_____ describes the bonding, orbital arrangement, and other characteristics of coordination complexes. It represents an application of molecular orbital theory to transition metal complexes. A transition metal ion has nine valence atomic orbitals - consisting of five nd, three p, and one s orbitals. These orbitals are of appropriate energy to form bonding interaction with ligands. The LFT analysis is highly dependent on the geometry of the complex, but most explanations begin by describing octahedral complexes, where six ligands coordinate to the metal. Other complexes can be described by reference to crystal field theory.

Exam Probability: **Medium**

34. *Answer choices:*

(see index for correct answer)

- a. Actinides in the environment
- b. Earth
- c. Chemical transport reaction
- d. Ligand field theory

Guidance: level 1

:: Functional groups ::

A _____ is a chemical derivative of phosphoric acid. The _____ ion is an inorganic chemical, the conjugate base that can form many different salts. In organic chemistry, a _____ , or organo _____ , is an ester of phosphoric acid. Of the various phosphoric acids and _____ s, organic _____ s are important in biochemistry and biogeochemistry , and inorganic _____ s are mined to obtain phosphorus for use in agriculture and industry. At elevated temperatures in the solid state, _____ s can condense to form pyro _____ s.

Exam Probability: **Low**

35. *Answer choices:*

(see index for correct answer)

- a. Phosphate
- b. Aziridine
- c. Oxaziridine
- d. Amide

Guidance: level 1

:: Carbenes ::

In chemistry, a _____ is a molecule containing a neutral carbon atom with a valence of two and two unshared valence electrons. The general formula is R--R' or R=C: where the R represent substituents or hydrogen atoms.

Exam Probability: **Low**

36. *Answer choices:*

(see index for correct answer)

- a. Carbene
- b. Methylene
- c. Persistent carbene
- d. Difluorocarbene

Guidance: level 1

:: Atomic physics ::

The _____ is a physical constant, approximately equal to the most probable distance between the nucleus and the electron in a hydrogen atom in its ground state. It is named after Niels Bohr, due to its role in the Bohr model of an atom. Its value is $5.2917721067 \times 10^{-11}$ m.

Exam Probability: **Low**

37. *Answer choices:*

(see index for correct answer)

- a. Quadrupole splitting
- b. Solid harmonics
- c. Principal quantum number
- d. Bohr radius

:: Hemoproteins ::

_____ s are a large family of enzymes which play a role in various biological processes.

Exam Probability: **Low**

38. *Answer choices:*

(see index for correct answer)

- a. Cytoglobin
- b. Methemoglobin
- c. Haem peroxidase
- d. Peroxidase

:: Cubic minerals ::

_____ is a chemical element with symbol Ag and atomic number 47. A soft, white, lustrous transition metal, it exhibits the highest electrical conductivity, thermal conductivity, and reflectivity of any metal. The metal is found in the Earth's crust in the pure, free elemental form , as an alloy with gold and other metals, and in minerals such as argentite and chlorargyrite. Most _____ is produced as a byproduct of copper, gold, lead, and zinc refining.

Exam Probability: **High**

39. *Answer choices:*

(see index for correct answer)

- a. Analcime
- b. Carlsbergite
- c. Silver
- d. Halite

Guidance: level 1

:: Atomic physics ::

In atomic theory and quantum mechanics, an _____ is a mathematical function that describes the wave-like behavior of either one electron or a pair of electrons in an atom. This function can be used to calculate the probability of finding any electron of an atom in any specific region around the atom's nucleus. The term _____ may also refer to the physical region or space where the electron can be calculated to be present, as defined by the particular mathematical form of the orbital.

40. *Answer choices:*

(see index for correct answer)

- a. Atomic orbital
- b. Boson
- c. Spherical harmonics
- d. Electron beam ion source

Guidance: level 1

:: Coordination chemistry ::

In inorganic chemistry, the _____ is the labilization of ligands that are trans to certain other ligands, which can thus be regarded as trans-directing ligands. It is attributed to electronic effects and it is most notable in square planar complexes, although it can also be observed for octahedral complexes. The cis effect is most often observed in octahedral transition metal complexes.

Exam Probability: **Low**

41. *Answer choices:*

(see index for correct answer)

- a. Dissociative substitution
- b. Ate complex

- c. Trans effect
- d. Hemilability

Guidance: level 1

:: Chemical elements ::

_____ is a chemical element with the symbol Zn and atomic number 30. _____ is a slightly brittle metal at room temperature and has a blue-silvery appearance when oxidation is removed. It is the first element in group 12 of the periodic table. In some respects _____ is chemically similar to magnesium: both elements exhibit only one normal oxidation state , and the Zn^{2+} and Mg^{2+} ions are of similar size. _____ is the 24th most abundant element in Earth's crust and has five stable isotopes. The most common _____ ore is sphalerite , a _____ sulfide mineral. The largest workable lodes are in Australia, Asia, and the United States. _____ is refined by froth flotation of the ore, roasting, and final extraction using electricity .

Exam Probability: **High**

42. *Answer choices:*

(see index for correct answer)

- a. Zirconium
- b. Zinc
- c. Flerovium
- d. Unbibium

:: Teratogens ::

_____ is an organic chemical compound with the chemical formula C6H6. The _____ molecule is composed of six carbon atoms joined in a ring with one hydrogen atom attached to each. As it contains only carbon and hydrogen atoms, _____ is classed as a hydrocarbon.

Exam Probability: **Low**

43. *Answer choices:*

(see index for correct answer)

- a. Benzene
- b. Cyclopamine
- c. N-Nitroso-N-methylurea
- d. Hexachlorophene

:: Cyanides ::

A _____ is a chemical compound that contains the group C=N. This group, known as the cyano group, consists of a carbon atom triple-bonded to a nitrogen atom.

Exam Probability: **Medium**

44. *Answer choices:*

(see index for correct answer)

- a. Barium cyanide
- b. Cyanide
- c. Cyanogen halide
- d. Cyanogen iodide

Guidance: level 1

:: Molecular physics ::

In chemistry, a _____ is a mathematical function describing the wave-like behavior of an electron in a molecule. This function can be used to calculate chemical and physical properties such as the probability of finding an electron in any specific region. The term orbital was introduced by Robert S. Mulliken in 1932 as an abbreviation for one-electron orbital wave function. At an elementary level, it is used to describe the region of space in which the function has a significant amplitude. _____ s are usually constructed by combining atomic orbitals or hybrid orbitals from each atom of the molecule, or other _____ s from groups of atoms. They can be quantitatively calculated using the Hartree–Fock or self-consistent field methods.

45. *Answer choices:*

(see index for correct answer)

- a. Macromolecular docking
- b. Gaussian orbital
- c. Molecular orbital
- d. Positronium hydride

Guidance: level 1

:: Concepts in physics ::

Whether electric or magnetic, _____ s can be characterized by their _____ moment, a vector quantity. For the simple electric _____ , the electric _____ moment points from the negative charge towards the positive charge, and has a magnitude equal to the strength of each charge times the separation between the charges.

Exam Probability: **Medium**

46. *Answer choices:*

(see index for correct answer)

- a. particle
- b. thermodynamic

- c. density function
- d. Dipole

Guidance: level 1

:: Nuclear materials ::

_____ is one of two stable isotopes of hydrogen . The nucleus of _____ , called a deuteron, contains one proton and one neutron, whereas the far more common protium has no neutron in the nucleus. _____ has a natural abundance in Earth's oceans of about one atom in 6420 of hydrogen. Thus _____ accounts for approximately 0.02% of all the naturally occurring hydrogen in the oceans, while protium accounts for more than 99.98%. The abundance of _____ changes slightly from one kind of natural water to another .

Exam Probability: **Low**

47. *Answer choices:*

(see index for correct answer)

- a. Deuterium
- b. Weapons-grade
- c. Tritiated water
- d. Ammonium uranyl carbonate

Guidance: level 1

:: Crystallography ::

In crystallography, the hexagonal crystal family is one of the 6 crystal families, which includes 2 crystal systems and 2 lattice systems .

Exam Probability: **Medium**

48. *Answer choices:*

(see index for correct answer)

- a. Wallpaper group
- b. Journal of Chemical Crystallography
- c. Stereographic projection
- d. Trigonal

Guidance: level 1

:: Cubic minerals ::

_____ is a chemical element with symbol Pt and atomic number 78. It is a dense, malleable, ductile, highly unreactive, precious, silverish-white transition metal. Its name is derived from the Spanish term platino, meaning "little silver".

Exam Probability: **Medium**

49. *Answer choices:*

(see index for correct answer)

- a. Brownleeite
- b. Coloradoite
- c. Gananite
- d. Domeykite

Guidance: level 1

:: Light-sensitive chemicals ::

_____ is a chemical compound with the formula H_2O_2. In its pure form, it is a pale blue, clear liquid, slightly more viscous than water. _____ is the simplest peroxide . It is used as an oxidizer, bleaching agent and antiseptic. Concentrated _____ , or "high-test peroxide", is a reactive oxygen species and has been used as a propellant in rocketry. Its chemistry is dominated by the nature of its unstable peroxide bond.

Exam Probability: **Low**

50. *Answer choices:*

(see index for correct answer)

- a. Lysergic acid diethylamide
- b. Potassium dichromate
- c. Ammonium dichromate
- d. Hydrogen peroxide

:: Chemical elements ::

_____ is a chemical element with symbol N and atomic number 7. It was first discovered and isolated by Scottish physician Daniel Rutherford in 1772. Although Carl Wilhelm Scheele and Henry Cavendish had independently done so at about the same time, Rutherford is generally accorded the credit because his work was published first. The name nitrogène was suggested by French chemist Jean-Antoine-Claude Chaptal in 1790, when it was found that _____ was present in nitric acid and nitrates. Antoine Lavoisier suggested instead the name azote, from the Greek t "no life", as it is an asphyxiant gas; this name is instead used in many languages, such as French, Russian, Romanian and Turkish, and appears in the English names of some _____ compounds such as hydrazine, azides and azo compounds.

Exam Probability: **Low**

51. *Answer choices:*

(see index for correct answer)

- a. Curium
- b. Cerium
- c. Einsteinium
- d. Nitrogen

:: Chemical elements ::

_____ is a chemical element with symbol Be and atomic number 4. It is a relatively rare element in the universe, usually occurring as a product of the spallation of larger atomic nuclei that have collided with cosmic rays. Within the cores of stars _____ is depleted as it is fused into heavier elements. It is a divalent element which occurs naturally only in combination with other elements in minerals. Notable gemstones which contain _____ include beryl and chrysoberyl. As a free element it is a steel-gray, strong, lightweight and brittle alkaline earth metal.

Exam Probability: **Low**

52. *Answer choices:*

(see index for correct answer)

- a. Tungsten
- b. Beryllium
- c. Systematic element name
- d. Transfermium Wars

Guidance: level 1

:: Chemical kinetics ::

The _____ of a chemical reaction is a particular configuration along the reaction coordinate. It is defined as the state corresponding to the highest potential energy along this reaction coordinate. At this point, assuming a perfectly irreversible reaction, colliding reactant molecules always go on to form products. It is often marked with the double dagger ‡ symbol.

Exam Probability: **High**

53. *Answer choices:*

(see index for correct answer)

- a. Stepwise reaction
- b. Receptor-ligand kinetics
- c. Transition state
- d. Activated complex

Guidance: level 1

:: Physical chemistry ::

In chemistry, a _____ is a special type of homogeneous mixture composed of two or more substances. In such a mixture, a solute is a substance dissolved in another substance, known as a solvent. The mixing process of a _____ happens at a scale where the effects of chemical polarity are involved, resulting in interactions that are specific to solvation. The _____ assumes the phase of the solvent when the solvent is the larger fraction of the mixture, as is commonly the case. The concentration of a solute in a _____ is the mass of that solute expressed as a percentage of the mass of the whole _____ . The term aqueous _____ is when one of the solvents is water.

54. *Answer choices:*

(see index for correct answer)

- a. Molar refractivity
- b. Conductivity
- c. Cubic harmonic
- d. Solution

Guidance: level 1

:: Phase transitions ::

_____ , or fusion, is a physical process that results in the phase transition of a substance from a solid to a liquid. This occurs when the internal energy of the solid increases, typically by the application of heat or pressure, which increases the substance's temperature to the _____ point. At the _____ point, the ordering of ions or molecules in the solid breaks down to a less ordered state, and the solid melts to become a liquid.

Exam Probability: **High**

55. *Answer choices:*

(see index for correct answer)

- a. Tricritical point
- b. Critical opalescence

- c. Melting
- d. Retrograde condensation

Guidance: level 1

:: Chelating agents ::

Denticity refers to the number of donor groups in a single ligand that bind to a central atom in a coordination complex. In many cases, only one atom in the ligand binds to the metal, so the denticity equals one, and the ligand is said to be _____ . Ligands with more than one bonded atom are called polydentate or multidentate. The word denticity is derived from dentis, the Latin word for tooth. The ligand is thought of as biting the metal at one or more linkage points. The denticity of a ligand is described with the Greek letter . For example, 6-EDTA describes an EDTA ligand that coordinates through 6 non-contiguous atoms.

Exam Probability: **High**

56. *Answer choices:*

(see index for correct answer)

- a. Penicillamine
- b. Monodentate
- c. Dimethylglyoxime
- d. Dimercaprol

Guidance: level 1

:: Quantum mechanics ::

In quantum mechanics, an _____ of a system is any quantum state of the system that has a higher energy than the ground state . Excitation is an elevation in energy level above an arbitrary baseline energy state. In physics there is a specific technical definition for energy level which is often associated with an atom being raised to an _____ . The temperature of a group of particles is indicative of the level of excitation .

Exam Probability: **High**

57. *Answer choices:*

(see index for correct answer)

- a. Quantum money
- b. Quantum hydrodynamics
- c. Finite potential well
- d. Quantum vacuum plasma thruster

Guidance: level 1

:: Anions ::

An oxide is a chemical compound that contains at least one oxygen atom and one other element in its chemical formula. "Oxide" itself is the dianion of oxygen, an O2– atom. Metal oxides thus typically contain an anion of oxygen in the oxidation state of -2. Most of the Earth's crust consists of solid oxides, the result of elements being oxidized by the oxygen in air or in water. Hydrocarbon combustion affords the two principal carbon oxides: carbon monoxide and carbon _____ . Even materials considered pure elements often develop an oxide coating. For example, aluminium foil develops a thin skin of Al2O3 that protects the foil from further corrosion. Individual elements can often form multiple oxides, each containing different amounts of the element and oxygen. In some cases these are distinguished by specifying the number of atoms as in carbon monoxide and carbon _____ , and in other cases by specifying the element's oxidation number, as in iron oxide and iron oxide. Certain elements can form many different oxides, such as those of nitrogen.

Exam Probability: **High**

58. *Answer choices:*

(see index for correct answer)

- a. Polyiodide
- b. Nitride
- c. Thiocyanate
- d. Dioxide

Guidance: level 1

:: Chemical bonding ::

A _____ in chemistry is a chemical bond between two chemical elements involving four bonding electrons instead of the usual two. The most common _____ occurs between two carbon atoms and can be found in alkenes. Many types of _____ s exist between two different elements. For example, in a carbonyl group with a carbon atom and an oxygen atom. Other common _____ s are found in azo compounds , imines and sulfoxides . In skeletal formula the _____ is drawn as two parallel lines between the two connected atoms; typographically, the equals sign is used for this. _____ s were first introduced in chemical notation by Russian chemist Alexander Butlerov.

Exam Probability: **High**

59. *Answer choices:*

(see index for correct answer)

- a. single bond
- b. Double bond
- c. MO diagram
- d. Electronegativity

Guidance: level 1

INDEX: Correct Answers

Fundamentals of Chemistry

1. : Nickel

2. c: Oxidation state

3. a: Dipole

4. d: Phenol

5. b: Chemical kinetics

6. : Lead

7. a: Metalloid

8. : Iodine

9. c: Acid

10. a: Perchloric acid

11. b: Citric acid

12. b: Solid

13. c: Glucose

14. d: Half-life

15. c: Ozone layer

16. c: Proton

17. a: Polymer

18. b: Subatomic particle

19. c: Radium

20. c: Binding energy

21. b: Aluminum

22. d: Crystal structure

23. d: Lewis acid

24. b: Photon

25. b: Noble gas

26. a: Hydrochloric acid

27. b: Principal quantum number

28. b: Spectroscopy

29. c: Diethyl ether

30. c: Ground state

31. d: Radioactive decay

32. : Electrolyte

33. d: Monosaccharide

34. c: Insulin

35. b: Distillation

36. b: Toluene

37. c: Sodium hydroxide

38. d: Alloy

39. d: Isotope

40. b: Endothermic

41. c: Lanthanide

42. d: Sucrose

43. d: Phosphorus

44. c: Oxidizing agent

45. d: Alkene

46. c: Enzyme

47. d: Calcium carbonate

48. d: Cholesterol

49. : Ionization energy

50. b: Alkali

51. b: Germanium

52. : Positron emission

53. c: Osmotic pressure

54. : Reducing agent

55. b: Oxygen

56. d: Evaporation

57. d: Sulfuric acid

58. b: Ether

59. : Ethylene glycol

Materials science

1. d: Polarizability

2. b: Dielectric

3. b: Hydrolysis

4. b: Photoresist

5. b: Reinforced concrete

6. b: Statically indeterminate

7. : Polyethylene

8. b: Hot working

9. c: Ring-opening polymerization

10. a: Homogeneous

11. b: Tensile strength

12. : Pultrusion

13. b: Raman spectroscopy

14. d: Enzyme

15. b: Reciprocal lattice

16. b: Glass-ceramic

17. c: Magnetization

18. d: Embrittlement

19. b: Crystal

20. a: Nondestructive testing

21. : Cooling curve

22. c: Ethylene glycol

23. a: Zeolite

24. a: Viscosity

25. c: Nanocomposite

26. a: Oxide

27. c: Tool steel

28. c: Magnesium

29. c: Hydrogen

30. d: Titanium alloy

31. : Diamond cubic

32. c: Brass

33. d: Chromium

34. a: Tacticity

35. d: Vulcanization

36. b: Water

37. c: Drift velocity

38. b: Grain boundary

39. a: Zinc

40. c: Nitriding

41. a: Fermi energy

42. c: Microscopy

43. : Polymer

44. c: Carbon

45. d: Electrolyte

46. d: Plasticizer

47. a: Bakelite

48. c: Ether

49. : Laser

50. b: Compton scattering

51. d: Organic compound

52. b: Pearlite

53. : Catalyst

54. b: Dendrite

55. a: Extrusion

56. : Polyethylene terephthalate

57. d: Goniometer

58. c: Polycarbonate

59. c: Electron

Analytical chemistry

1. a: Standard addition

2. : Pervaporation

3. b: Atomic orbital

4. a: Sodium

5. b: Hydrazine

6. b: Reference electrode

7. c: Benzoic acid

8. a: Sugar

9. a: Mixture

10. d: Solubility

11. d: Masking agent

12. d: Steroid

13. d: Crystal

14. b: Iron

15. d: Acetone

16. a: Perturbation theory

17. b: Gel electrophoresis

18. c: Gas laws

19. c: Graphite

20. c: Reducing agent

21. a: Ionization

22. : Nitrate

23. d: Crown ether

24. b: Antimony

25. : Potentiometric titration

26. a: Mass transfer

27. : Cation

28. : Spectroscopy

29. d: Distillation

30. a: Nucleic acid

31. a: Light scattering

32. b: Mineral

33. c: Carbonyl

34. c: Chemical ionization

35. c: Ether

36. : Oxidation state

37. c: Detection limit

38. c: Ammonium

39. d: Titration

40. a: Membrane

41. d: Carbonate

42. c: Ester

43. d: Iodine

44. a: Reversed-phase chromatography

45. a: Molarity

46. : Atomic spectroscopy

47. c: Eigenfunction

48. b: Cerium

49. : Electrolysis

50. b: Standard hydrogen electrode

51. : Vapor pressure

52. : Capillary electrophoresis

53. b: Micelle

54. a: Absorption spectrum

55. : Affinity chromatography

56. : Infrared spectroscopy

57. : Assay

58. a: Organic acid

59. : Glucose

Organic chemistry

1. c: Alkyl halides

2. b: Citric acid

3. d: Halide

4. : Carbonic acid

5. a: Toluene

6. c: Pyridine

7. c: Nitronium ion

8. b: Bond length

9. b: Salt

10. a: Physical property

11. c: Reaction coordinate

12. : Ketone

13. b: Solution

14. : Progesterone

15. d: Cyclopentane

16. c: Peroxide

17. c: Glycolysis

18. : Glycoside

19. b: Aldol condensation

20. d: Diastereomer

21. c: Hydrolysis

22. b: Cellulose

23. : Grignard reagents

24. b: Urea

25. d: Dimethyl sulfoxide

26. c: Hemiacetal

27. b: Inductive effect

28. c: Phosphorus tribromide

29. : Stereochemistry

30. d: Polymer

31. c: Robinson annulation

32. d: Crown ether

33. c: Cyclohexanol

34. b: 1-Bromobutane

35. c: Organic reaction

36. a: Hammett equation

37. b: Dipole

38. a: Lipid

39. c: Carbanion

40. : Electrophilic substitution

41. b: Exothermic reaction

42. : Benzyl

43. a: Ionization

44. b: Glycerol

45. a: Carbocation

46. b: Aniline

47. a: Oleic acid

48. b: Addition reaction

49. a: Succinic acid

50. : Pyrrole

51. a: Vinyl chloride

52. d: Fischer projection

53. a: Sodium borohydride

54. : Acyl halide

55. d: Alanine

56. d: Sulfide

57. : Clemmensen Reduction

58. d: Haloalkane

59. c: Amide

Physical chemistry

1. b: Atomic number

2. d: Curie

3. c: Absorbance

4. c: Fermion

5. d: Transition state

6. a: Calcium

7. d: Phase problem

8. a: Resonance

9. d: Bohr magneton

10. c: Enzyme kinetics

11. c: Gas constant

12. : Potassium

13. c: Vapor pressure

14. b: Flash photolysis

15. c: Slater-type orbital

16. : Glass electrode

17. d: Perfect gas

18. c: Iron

19. a: Nitrogen

20. c: Real gas

21. : Melting

22. c: Ground state

23. : Principal quantum number

24. a: Meissner effect

25. d: Rate-determining step

26. b: Helium

27. d: Gas laws

28. d: Isolated system

29. : Polymer

30. a: Equilibrium constant

31. a: Hydroxide

32. b: Reaction quotient

33. d: Polarizability

34. b: Wavelength

35. a: Electron transfer

36. a: Bohr radius

37. d: Vanadium

38. a: Spectrometer

39. a: Thermodynamic equilibrium

40. d: Graphite

41. c: Slater determinant

42. c: Differential scanning calorimetry

43. : Base pair

44. a: Oscillator strength

45. : Morse potential

46. a: Exothermic reaction

47. c: Partial pressure

48. b: Stark effect

49. b: Permittivity

50. d: Vibrational temperature

51. b: Sulfide

52. : Monochromator

53. b: Chemical kinetics

54. b: Quantum yield

55. : Ammonia

56. d: Lyman series

57. d: Speed of light

58. a: Acid

59. d: Collision frequency

Chemical engineering

1. d: Heat flux

2. a: Pollution prevention

3. c: Sedimentation

4. a: Aeration

5. a: Condensation

6. a: Drying

7. b: Thin film

8. : Brinkman number

9. a: Homogeneous catalysis

10. c: Monooxygenase

11. c: Collision theory

12. a: Dust explosion

13. : Fermentation

14. : Cryogenics

15. b: Chromium

16. b: Cooling tower

17. b: Instability

18. c: Methanol

19. b: Enol

20. a: Solution

21. b: Allyl

22. : Walden inversion

23. : Enol ether

24. b: Green chemistry

25. : Incineration

26. d: Separation process

27. : Refrigeration

28. c: Biogas

29. a: Acrylate

30. b: Electrolyte

31. d: Robinson annulation

32. d: Butane

33. d: Cyclohexane

34. c: Ammonia

35. d: Amino acid

36. a: Biocatalysis

37. : Reboiler

38. b: Sharpless epoxidation

39. d: Hydraulics

40. a: Marangoni effect

41. a: Protease

42. d: Chemical potential

43. b: Fractionation

44. d: Polymer

45. b: Ion exchange

46. a: Hydrogen peroxide

47. a: Epoxide

48. c: Benzylamine

49. c: Enzyme

50. d: Nozzle

51. c: Adsorption

52. d: Supercritical fluid

53. d: Converting

54. b: Benzene

55. a: Styrene

56. b: Contact angle

57. b: Quinine

58. c: Convection

59. c: Methane

Inorganic chemistry

1. a: Fluorine

2. c: Physical property

3. d: Gallium

4. b: Lewis base

5. d: Metallic bonding

6. a: Nernst equation

7. d: Phosphorous acid

8. d: Aqua regia

9. a: Triple bond

10. b: Hemerythrin

11. b: Crystal field theory

12. d: Portland cement

13. b: Mineral

14. b: Electrolysis

15. d: Latimer diagram

16. c: Amino acid

17. : Potassium chloride

18. a: Iodine

19. c: Reaction rate

20. b: Acetylide

21. b: Solvay process

22. d: Nitric oxide

23. a: Orbital theory

24. b: Principal quantum number

25. c: Hemoglobin

26. c: Metal carbonyl

27. c: Cisplatin

28. d: Hybrid orbitals

29. b: Ferredoxin

30. : Carborane

31. : D-block

32. : Phosphorus

33. d: Zirconium

34. d: Ligand field theory

35. a: Phosphate

36. a: Carbene

37. d: Bohr radius

38. d: Peroxidase

39. c: Silver

40. a: Atomic orbital

41. c: Trans effect

42. b: Zinc

43. a: Benzene

44. b: Cyanide

45. c: Molecular orbital

46. d: Dipole

47. a: Deuterium

48. d: Trigonal

49. : Platinum

50. d: Hydrogen peroxide

51. d: Nitrogen

52. b: Beryllium

53. c: Transition state

54. d: Solution

55. c: Melting

56. b: Monodentate

57. : Excited state

58. d: Dioxide

59. b: Double bond

CPSIA information can be obtained
at www.ICGtesting.com
Printed in the USA
LVHW062137311019
635718LV00025B/563/P